Glasgow
40 Town and Country Walks

The author and publisher have made every effort to ensure that the information in this publication is accurate, and accept no responsibility whatsoever for any loss, injury or inconvenience experienced by any person or persons whilst using this book.

published by
pocket mountains ltd
6 Church Wynd, Bo'ness EH51 0AN
pocketmountains.com

ISBN-13: 978-0-9554548-1-3

Text copyright © John Craig and Katie Smith 2008

Photography copyright © Robbie Porteous 2008

The right of John Craig and Katie Smith to be identified as the Authors of this work has been asserted by them in accordance with the Copyright, Designs and Patents Act 1988

A catalogue record for this book is available from the British Library

Printed in Poland

Introduction

Glasgow is Scotland's largest and arguably most cosmopolitan city, renowned for its brilliant mix of nightlife, shopping and culture – in particular art and architecture – as well as its distinctive humour. With beautiful parks and gardens to be found all over the city and unrivalled access to some of Scotland's most spectacular countryside, it is also easy to see why Glasgow is known to many as the Dear Green Place. Within an hour from the city centre, you can be climbing one of the peaks that surround Loch Lomond or making a start on the West Highland Way, which begins just north of the city and ends in Fort William.

Even closer to home are the hill ranges that form a rim around Glasgow, from the distinctive lava scarps of the Campsie Fells north of the city to the less-visited Kilpatrick Hills and Renfrewshire Heights in the west. There are many great viewpoints across the city to be found in these hills, while views from within the city itself are accentuated by the steep, elongated drumlins (glacial deposits) on which many of the streets are built.

How to use this guide
Taking from just 30 minutes to just over three hours, the 40 walks in this book are extremely varied and many include optional detours, allowing you to extend the route, or visit points of historical and cultural interest that can, if desired, turn an hour-long route into a half or full day out. Almost all of the walks are circular and accessible by public transport from the city centre, and many contain refreshment stops and family facilities.

A sketch map accompanies each route. Many are waymarked or well-trodden enough for there to be little chance of getting lost, but for navigation on some hill routes in remoter areas carrying an OS map and compass is advised.

Approximate distances and timescales are given for general guidance, but in many cases you may want to allow longer to visit points of interest en route. As a broad guide, one hour has been allowed for every 4km, with extra time built in for ascent and rough ground.

The routes have been divided up into five regions. The first chapter, in particular, demonstrates how you can incorporate the best of the city sights in just a few short walks. It also features the green spaces that offer a welcome, and often idyllic, respite from the bustle of one of Europe's most exciting cities.

Travelling west along the Clyde into the hills above the great former shipbuilding areas is a region of high, remote moorland, rich in both ecological value and ancient history with engaging views over Greater Glasgow. Here, you'll find Clyde Muirshiel Regional Park, which encompasses many of the walks in the second chapter.

Heading north over the River Clyde, the third chapter takes you on a journey of great diversity – from the rugged wilderness plateau of the Kilpatrick Hills to the waterfront at Helensburgh and the banks of Loch Lomond at the heart of Scotland's first national park.

Turning east, you reach the hill range most commonly associated with Glasgow – the Campsie Fells – whose sheer south face forms a dramatic backdrop to the city. The fourth chapter features a number of relatively small but still rugged and challenging hills in this range, with some more level walks with views of the Campsies along the start of the West Highland Way in Mugdock Country Park. Other walks take in the Antonine Wall and Forth & Clyde Canal in the Kelvin Valley, which runs along the foot of the Campsies, and a famous battlesite adjacent to the family-friendly Colzium Estate just outside Kilsyth.

The final chapter explores some of the most interesting and accessible walking areas that Lanarkshire and the Clyde Valley, south of Glasgow, have to offer. Many of these are in country parks whose attractions range from natural features such as waterfalls, gorges, lochs and woods to entertainment in the form of boating ponds, walled gardens, children's farms and waymarked nature trails.

Countryside access

Since the arrival of the Land Reform (Scotland) Act, which establishes a public right of access to most land and inland water, Scotland is regarded as having the best access arrangements in Europe, if not the world. While most of the walks in this volume follow established routes frequented by walkers, you should still make yourself familiar with the responsibilities set out in the Scottish Outdoor Access Code. Some key points are to avoid damage to fences and crops and close all gates properly on farmland, take all your litter home with you and do not light fires anywhere in the countryside.

Dog walkers should keep dogs on a leash by reservoirs, playparks and livestock and should avoid entering any field where there are young animals, while on open ground dogs must be kept on a tight leash and wary distance during lambing (March to May) and ground-nesting (April to July). Always clear up after your dog in any public space, not just in city parks.

Walking with children

Many of these routes have been designed with families in mind and the best-equipped country parks, in particular, provide great opportunities for walking with younger children and buggies, as well as offering facilities and refreshments (though be aware some might be seasonal). However, uneven surfaces make all-terrain buggies the only really practical option for any of the walks indicated as being pushchair-friendly.

Some of these walks offer an ideal

introduction to small hills for older children, but make sure any route you do is within the capability of the youngest member of your group and that you let them set the pace. Success in encouraging children to walk is more likely if you select varied routes with plenty of interesting features, plants and animals to spot and, of course, ensure they are wearing comfortable footwear and clothing and have plenty of refreshments.

Safety
Glasgow is surrounded by very accessible small hills that give good views over the city and beyond – many for relatively little effort. Almost half of the routes in this volume either take one of these hills as their focal point or offer optional detours to viewpoints.

Although most offer much easier and more accessible alternatives to the higher peaks, particularly in winter, it is wise to avoid any hill walk in really bad weather or limited daylight and always take the relevant map and compass with you where an OS map number is indicated in the route text.

Be aware that there may be crags or serious drops if you wander off-route, and for longer, remoter challenges, a warm, waterproof layer and proper footwear is a must. While many of the lower-level country strolls featured also make for great winter walking, take care after heavy rain and, again, always wear appropriate

footwear with good grips, especially along riversides and gorges.

Transport
Almost all of these walks are circular, usually returning to the start point on foot but occasionally making use of public transport to complete the loop. Wherever possible, routes have been devised to start and finish at points accessible by public transport.

Frequent trains run from Glasgow's Central and Queen Street Stations to a number of the destinations featured in this guide (*firstgroup.com/scotrail*) while the Glasgow Subway connects sites closer to the city centre (*spt.co.uk/subway*).

For walks not on the rail network, there is often fairly direct bus access from the city centre – though you may need to build in time for the approach walk.

One of the main bus providers for the Glasgow area is Strathclyde Passenger Transport, which also provides the Ring'n'Ride service to areas that have no direct bus service: anyone can use the service but you do need to register and book in advance (*spt.co.uk/bus*).

Other providers include First Glasgow (*firstgroup.com/ukbus/scotland/swscot*), Scottish Citylink (*citylink.co.uk*) and McColl's (*mccolls.org.uk*).

Additional public transport information for routes in this book can be found from the very helpful Traveline Scotland (*travelinescotland.com*).

Post-industrial Glasgow is one of the world's most successful reinventions – cosmopolitan, buzzing, stylish – all in a setting of fabulous Victorian architecture with some of the most renowned cultural venues and one of the richest city art collections in Europe.

But it is also known as the Dear Green Place (from the Gaelic *Glaschu*), a name that remains as relevant today as it has always been, with its tree-lined avenues, glorious gardens and more public parks than any other city of its size.

This chapter focuses on the inescapable sense of history and the wealth of architecture and art, as well as the dear green spaces, that are to be found in this great city. You'll find yourself in pursuit of some of the finest buildings in Scotland

on the Mackintosh Trail, discovering one of Britain's great Victorian parks on a tour of the West End and travelling back through the Merchant City's fascinating history as you explore the Necropolis and Glasgow Green.

Further out from the city's bustling centre, there are some glorious pockets of peace and quiet waiting to be discovered. Two of Glasgow's largest parks – Pollok, home to the world-famous Burrell Collection, and Linn Park, with its shady riverside walkway, feature in this chapter as does tranquil Dawsholm Park in the north of the city and Rouken Glen, a wonderful Southside haven.

All of these circular walks start from or are accessible from the city centre with a short hop on the tube, bus or train.

City Trails and Dear Green Places

On the Mackintosh Trail

Distance 4.5km **Time** 1 hour
Terrain paved, mostly level
Access subway to Hillhead; return from
Buchanan Street Underground Station

**This route includes so many treasures,
including Glasgow University and several
wonderful buildings designed by Charles
Rennie Mackintosh, that you could easily
make a full day of it.**

Start at Hillhead Underground Station
on Byres Road, the hub of the West End.
From the exit, turn left down Byres Road
and first left into Ashton Lane, home to
some great pubs and restaurants. Turn
right to continue down the lane and take
the path on the left up a flight of steps
into the campus of Glasgow University.
Founded in 1451, its Gothic spires have
dominated the West End skyline since the
1870s. With the Main Building on the hill
ahead, pass Queen Margaret Union on
your left as you go along University
Gardens and left onto University Avenue.

On your left here, up from the traffic
lights, is the Hunterian Museum and Art
Gallery and Mackintosh House. The latter
– a reconstruction of the home of famed
architect Charles Rennie Mackintosh
– is signified by a bizarre door halfway
up the outside wall of the building at
78 Southpark Terrace and can be accessed
for a fee via the Hunterian Museum.
The Museum itself is free.

Cross University Avenue at the traffic
lights to enter the University's Main Gate
and Main Building and continue straight
ahead through the arched cloisters and
out of the building for views across the
city. From the flagpole, go left to a flight
of steps where the road bends. You can
usually get straight down to the tree-lined
Kelvin Way and Kelvingrove Park from
here, but if you find the gate on the steps
locked, go back to University Avenue, turn
right down the hill and right again at the
traffic island onto Kelvin Way.

Access Kelvingrove Park near the top of

◀ The Glasgow School
of Art on Renfrew Street

Kelvin Way, adjacent to the University.
Once in the park, pass a statue of Thomas
Carlyle and cross the bridge over the River
Kelvin to take the main path on the right.
When this splits, keep to the one closest
to the side of the hill and follow it past
the Stewart Memorial Fountain, ignoring
a couple of turn-offs on your left to meet
the long shrub-lined boulevard which
takes you to the exit.

Go straight down the terraces of
Clairmont Gardens and Woodside Place to
reach the M8 pedestrian bridge. After
crossing, follow the curved path to your
left to emerge onto Buccleuch Street by
The Tenement House, home to shorthand
typist Miss Agnes Toward from 1911 to
1965 and now in the care of the National
Trust for Scotland.

Continuing up Buccleuch Street, take
the first right uphill onto Garnet Street,
then left onto Renfrew Street to the
Glasgow School of Art with the imposing
Mackintosh Building unmistakably on
your right. As Renfrew Street dips
downhill, the famous Glasgow Film
Theatre appears just beside you on Rose
Street. Pass the GFT and turn left down
Sauchiehall Street, keeping an eye
out for another of Mackintosh's
landmarks – the Willow Tea Rooms on

the first floor at
217 Sauchiehall Street.

Further on, you'll
come to the Royal Concert Hall and the
statue of Scotland's first First Minister,
Donald Dewar. Turn down Buchanan
Street and, as you near the bottom, you'll
see Mackintosh's second Willow Tea
Rooms, at number 97.

A short detour soon after on your right
takes you down the narrow Mitchell Lane
to another Mackintosh landmark, his
Glasgow Herald building, now the 'art and
architecture platform' The Lighthouse.

Return up Buchanan Street to head into
Royal Exchange Square via Exchange
Place. The big building in the centre is
GOMA – Glasgow Museum of Modern Art
– the second most visited contemporary
art gallery outside London. Turning left
up Queen Street, you soon pass the heart
of the city, George Square, with its statues
and City Chambers. To make a circuit of
the walk, take the underground from
Buchanan Street back to Hillhead.

Kelvingrove and the West End

Distance 5km Time 1 hour Terrain paved and level Access subway from any city centre tube stop to Hillhead Underground Station

A walk that offers views over the West End from Kelvingrove Park, a tour of Kelvingrove Art Gallery and a wander through the beautiful Botanic Gardens.

Start at Hillhead Underground Station on the main West End thoroughfare, Byres Road. Turn left down Byres Road from the exit and carry on until you see Church Street on your left, which brings you onto Dumbarton Road. Bear left along this, crossing the bridge over the River Kelvin. Here you get your first views of the impressive Kelvingrove Art Gallery and Museum, home to one of the best civic art collections in Europe.

Unless you plan to spend some time in the Art Gallery and Museum, take the path just before the building which passes round 'the back' to the driveway and out onto tree-lined Kelvin Way. The bridge just to your left boasts four remarkable pairs of sculpture, which depict War and Peace, Navigation and Shipbuilding, Philosophy and Inspiration, and Commerce and Industry. This bridge was bombed during the Second World War and, appropriately, War sustained the most damage. From the bridge, cross Kelvin Way into the principal section of Kelvingrove Park, designed by Sir Joseph Paxton of Crystal Palace fame. Ahead on the left, you pass a small skatepark before coming to the iconic Stewart Memorial Fountain ahead. It commemorates the development of the Loch Katrine water system, which supplies the city, and was inspired by Sir Walter Scott's poem, *The Lady of the Lake*.

From here, head uphill to the statue of a tiger and cubs, passing immediately left

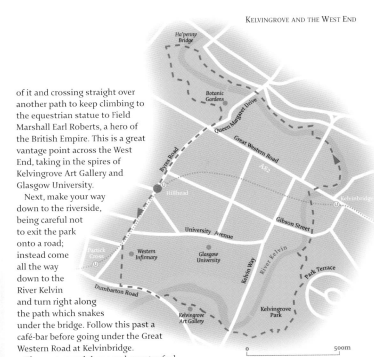

of it and crossing straight over another path to keep climbing to the equestrian statue to Field Marshall Earl Roberts, a hero of the British Empire. This is a great vantage point across the West End, taking in the spires of Kelvingrove Art Gallery and Glasgow University.

Next, make your way down to the riverside, being careful not to exit the park onto a road; instead come all the way down to the River Kelvin and turn right along the path which snakes under the bridge. Follow this past a café-bar before going under the Great Western Road at Kelvinbridge.

The next stretch has a real country feel in the midst of the city. After walking under the grand Belmont Street bridge and the Queen Margaret Drive bridge, you'll pass an iron bridge on your left. Soon after, you come to the Ha'penny Bridge House, where tolls were once collected for crossing the Kelvin, and the Ha'penny Bridge itself.

Cross this and follow the road uphill to the left and the first entrance into the Botanic Gardens. Many exotic species of plant can be found here and the orchid collection is especially worth seeing. The restored Kibble Palace is a fantastic example of Victorian ironwork greenhouse design and the surrounding lawns a great favourite with locals in the summer months. Take the main exit out of the gardens, just past the Kibble Palace, to the busy crossroads at the top of Byres Road. Carry on down this thoroughfare to return to Hillhead Underground Station and the start of your walk.

◀ Kelvingrove Art Gallery and Museum from Kelvin Way

The Necropolis and Glasgow Green

**Distance 7km Time 2 hours, but allow
plenty of time to explore the Necropolis
Terrain paved but with some uphill
stretches Access trains and buses to
Queen Street Station**

**A tour of some of the oldest parts of
the city, including the Cathedral, the
Necropolis, Glasgow Green, the People's
Palace and the Clyde.**

Starting from Queen Street Station,
head south down Queen Street, passing
George Square and the grand City
Chambers that form the heart of the city
on your left. When you are level with the
Gallery of Modern Art, turn left onto
Ingram Street. To your right is the
redeveloped Merchant City, once the
commercial and social hub for the traders
who had by the late 19th century made
Glasgow the Second City of the Empire.

At the next big junction, take a left
uphill onto High Street which soon
after becomes Castle Street. After a

few minutes you'll come to Provand's
Lordship, the oldest house in Glasgow
(1471), on the left and the fascinating
St Mungo Museum of Religious Life and
Art on the other side of the road. The big
attraction here, though, is Glasgow
Cathedral, one of only a few medieval
Scottish churches to survive the
Reformation intact.

Just south of the cathedral, you'll find a
large gate and access driveway to the
Necropolis, Glasgow's hilltop cemetery
where hundreds of monuments – many
designed by the leading architects of the
day – compete in scale and grandeur. After
crossing the ornate Bridge of Sighs, turn
left, then second right, climbing uphill to
enter the main section of the graveyard.
The statue of John Knox, leader of the
Reformation, towers above the
increasingly dramatic assemblage of
sculpture and architecture as sweeping
views over the city also unfold. Due to
the bewildering number of monuments

to see here, it is best to wander at will, using the Knox statue – the highest column in the Necropolis – to find your return route. Other landmarks as you descend include the intricate sandstone Major Archibald Douglas Monteath mausoleum. Head towards the cathedral to exit.

Retrace your steps back down High Street but, instead of turning onto Ingram Street, carry on down to Glasgow Cross and the landmark Tolbooth Steeple at the junction with the Trongate. Continue straight on under the railway to reach the Saltmarket and Glasgow Green, the city's oldest park, which can be accessed by Jocelyn Gate on the left.

Head towards the needle-like Nelson's Monument at the heart of Glasgow Green. On your left are the Winter Gardens, a huge Victorian glasshouse at the back of the People's Palace. Glasgow's social history museum is well worth a visit, as is

the terracotta Doulton Fountain at the front of the building. Adjacent to it is the lavish red-brick Templeton Carpet Factory.

At the access point for the Winter Gardens, you'll find a large circular mosaic waymarker at your feet: from here, head for the river, noting the Trafalgar Monument on your right and suspension bridge on your left before crossing another circular installation. Go right, and then left just before the arch to follow the path closest to the river.

Cross the main road into Clyde Street and continue on this road until you see a walkway on your left which takes you back to the Clyde and under the St Andrew's suspension footbridge (1856).

When you see La Pasionaria Memorial, a sculpture of a woman with raised arms which commemorates the British volunteers who died in the Spanish Civil War, return to the road (still Clyde Street). Cross into Dixon Street and through St Enoch Square to reach Buchanan Street. Follow this all the way up to West George Street where you turn right to Queen Street Station.

◀ The Templeton Carpet Factory

13

The Burrell and Pollok Park

Distance 5km **Time** 1 hour 30
Terrain level paths throughout, mostly
tarmac but some muddy sections
(steps by Pollok House) **Access** train
from Glasgow Central to Pollokshaws
West Station

A circuit of the only country park within
the city boundary, taking in the world-
renowned Burrell Collection, the
18th-century Pollok House which has its
own art collection and walled gardens
and the White Cart Water.

Start at the main entrance to Pollok
Park, off the B769 Pollokshaws Road, a
two-minute walk from Pollokshaws West
Station. Head up the start of the long
drive which leads to Pollok House
(signposted). Near the tennis courts,
a tarmac path forks right towards the
Burrell Collection (also signposted).
You soon cross another main drive, where
you'll see a car park on the left and the
Burrell Collection above right. Built in
the 1980s to house one of the greatest
collections of art held by a single person
in the world, it includes works by Degas
and Cezanne as well as vast medieval
tapestries, all gifted by Sir William Burrell
and his wife to the city in 1944.

After continuing past the Burrell on
your right, the path starts to climb. Keep
right at the two junctions that come in
quick succession by the sandstone
Knowehead Lodge to descend slightly,
soon passing an open space known as the
Glade on your left, where you fork right
under a canopy of fine mixed trees, left to
stay on the main path at the next fork and
left again at the next two junctions.

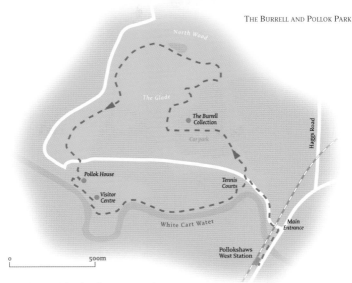

0   500m

Going straight ahead at a crossroads, you now pass a big pond with several little islands on your right before coming to a larger tarmac road which you turn left onto, heading gently downhill before contouring right past a sculpted wooden 'kissing' bench to eventually reach Pollok House.

Although it is a little overshadowed by its famous neighbour, this grand 18th-century mansion is well worth a visit. Now in the care of the National Trust for Scotland, it is home to some precious art, including works by Goya and the artist and poet William Blake, a fantastic library with many books on botany (you'll find more than 1000 varieties of rhododendron in the surrounding parkland), and a café

historically located in the old kitchens. The nearby walled and woodland gardens are also worth exploring.

From the car park beside the entrance to Pollok House, turn left up a short flight of steps to skirt round the house before crossing the front lawns towards the White Cart Water. After passing a picturesque old stone bridge over the river, loop around the right-hand side of the Old Stable Courtyard and past a dramatic weir and a wildlife garden to continue on the main riverside path, signed 'way out'. This passes fields, which are home to some Highland cattle, and a cricket ground. Soon after skirting around the tennis courts, turn right onto the main drive to return to the entrance.

Rouken Glen ramble

**Distance 3km Time 1 hour Terrain tarmac
paths and good nature trail; walkway
section suitable for buggies and trikes,
although steps to negotiate in places
Access bus (38A) from Union Street to
Rouken Glen Road or train from Glasgow
Central to Whitecraigs (starting route at
midway point by boating lake)**

**An ideal family day out in Giffnock's
Rouken Glen Park with its trike-friendly
tarmac walkways, boating pond and
waterside café, returning by a wilder
wooded glen and striking waterfall.**

Officially opened in 1906, Rouken Glen
is a mix of classic highlights that you
would expect of an Edwardian city park,
including bandstand and boating lake,
and more recent additions such as the
garden centre, Chinese restaurant and
art gallery – but it is the waterfall and

steep woodland that make it especially
rewarding for the walker.

It can get busy here at the weekends but
Rouken Glen – which is said to take its
name from the old Rock End Meal Mill in
the glen – is plenty large enough for you
to find your own quiet space.

Start at the park entrance on Rouken
Glen Road in Giffnock and follow the
main driveway to find a tarmac walkway
(one of many that are perfect for little
bikes, trikes and scooters) near a sign for
the Walkaboutabit Trail at the upper left
corner of the garden centre car park. Head
out past an information board into an
open setting of lawns, mature trees
and a playpark.

Turn right along the walkway
signposted Walled Garden, ignoring the
actual turn-off for the garden (as you pass
this later) to keep to the main walkway as

◀ Rouken Glen boating lake

it skirts round the big green to your left. About halfway round, come off to the right, by a sign for the pond and café to carry straight along a smaller path past more open green spaces.

Continue to follow signs for the pond and café which, after a gentle uphill stretch on a smaller path, is a lovely spot to relax and enjoy an ice-cream at one of the picnic benches, with paddleboats for hire from the small jetty in summer.

Walk clockwise around the tree-fringed pond and when you reach the corner opposite the café, leave the waterside by the track on the left: if in doubt, the dramatic sound of the waterfall ahead should guide you. The initial drop of this waterfall may come as a surprise for the size of the park and its proximity to the city. After crossing the bridge above it, go down the steps to the right to reach the bottom of the falls, framed beautifully by the arch of the bridge.

Descend into the wooded glen, noting the sign for Glen Walks as you follow the Auldhouse Burn downstream, crossing back and forth by a series of wooden bridges. After the third bridge, you start to climb uphill above the river to accompany an old stone wall for a while.

Soon after this ends, climb a short flight of stone steps and shortly turn right away from the Glen Walks sign to return to the network of tarmac walkways in the more open part of the park. Rejoin the main walkway around the large green, passing the Walled Garden on your left and a big stone gate with a clock above it. Take the next turning to the left to reach the car park and return to the start.

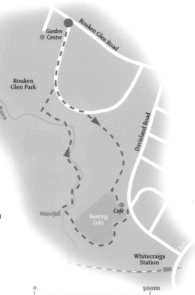

Linn Park and the White Cart

Distance 4km **Time** 1 hour
Terrain undulating route with several
flights of steps but good waymarked paths
throughout **Access** bus (44) from Union
Street to Clarkston Road or train from
Glasgow Central to Muirend or Cathcart

**This riverside loop along the White Cart
Walkway is easy to follow and offers a
quick getaway in the city's second largest
public park.**

Start by Netherlee Primary School and
Community Library, just off Clarkston
Road, Netherlee, which is between
Giffnock and Cathcart in the southeast of
the city and easily reached by bus. For
those approaching by train, disembark at
Cathcart Station to start the route at Snuff
Mill Bridge at the halfway point of the

walk described here, or Muirend Station, a
few minutes' walk from Netherlee School.

The walk can also be extended by a
visit to Alexander 'Greek' Thomson's
Holmwood House, built in the 1850s
and now owned by the National Trust
for Scotland. It can be found south of
Cathcart on the west side of the White
Cart Water.

From the car park by Netherlee
Primary, head away from Clarkston Road
to pick up a small path leading along a
fence on the edge of a small housing
estate and past a play area, before
entering pleasant woodland.

At a T-junction, turn left down some
steps and left again at the bottom to pass
behind the houses. The White Cart Water
– which originates in Eaglesham, East

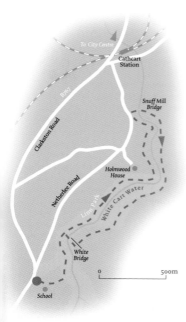

a waterfall. (For a closer look, go down some steps to reach a lovely level area at the bottom of the falls.)

Continue by this waymarked path as it undulates through the wooded glen, before descending a flight of steps to a sign for Snuff Mill Bridge. From here, a path with a wooden rail drops gradually down to water level before climbing several flights of steps again. A final set of steps takes you onto Snuff Mill Bridge and the pretty conservation area that surrounds it. This 18th-century stone bridge was once the only crossing on the White Cart Water. A sign points to Pollok House and Cathcart Station, the alternative start point for rail travellers.

After crossing the bridge and admiring the old buildings, turn right to re-enter Linn Park at an iron gate after around 20m. As you follow the east bank back along the river, keep to the path closest to the water (still marked with the green arrow all the way) as it crosses pleasant lawns backed by lovely mature trees before rising high above the water. At a bollard, follow the arrow straight ahead down a small dirt path to drop back to the riverside, ignoring the tarmac walkway which continues away over the lawns.

Keep to the right-hand path at the next two forks to come out on a tarmac road. Turn right downhill, following the rushing of the river as you pass more lawns and specimen trees on your journey back to the White Bridge. Cross this and turn left to retrace your steps to the start.

Renfrewshire and meanders through Linn Park and Pollok Country Park before flowing to Paisley – soon appears through the trees on your right.

As you head into dense woodland, keep to the main path to come out on a road: a sign points back the way you've come to Netherlee. Turn right onto this drive to pass the White Bridge, continuing on the west bank by a tarmac path marked by a green arrow, where you'll soon pass

◄ The White Bridge in Linn Park

Garscube Estate and Dawsholm Park

Distance 4km Time **1 hour** Terrain **300m
section of busy road with no pavement,
then paths and trails that can be muddy;
mostly level** Access **train from Glasgow
Queen Street to Kelvindale**

**This circuit along the River Kelvin
and through the nature-rich woodland
of Dawsholm Park and grounds of
Glasgow University Veterinary School
offers a great escape in a busy part of
the city. If you are a fan of unusual
rhododendrons or exotic trees, keep
your eyes peeled.**

After leaving Kelvindale train station on
Cleveden Road, bear left to make your way
up and along Dalsholm Road, passing a
recycling centre. Carry on down the road
and through the traffic barriers to enter
woodland and reach a stone bridge over
the River Kelvin. Turn left to go uphill
and, after around 50m, you'll see a big gap
in a stone wall: this is very much the

estate's 'back door'! Go through this for a
steep but short descent to pick up the
path that rises to the right in a hairpin
bend before carrying you above the river
through a mix of mature beech, yew,
oak and rhododendron.

The thrum of the traffic just metres
away behind the sandstone wall on
Maryhill Road heightens the feeling of
secrecy here. Take care as the path is
rather overgrown and indistinct in places:
at the first Y-junction, after around 300m,
take the left branch that leads downhill
by steps and, at the second, take the lower
option to continue above the river. Some
200m after the path contours right, it
comes out at a fence on the perimeter of

the rugby grounds. Turn immediately left towards the river and then right to follow the Kelvin upstream to join a tarmac path leading to the stately Lady Campbell Bridge. This is a lovely stretch, worlds away from the busy north Glasgow streets, with an abundance of wildflowers right through to autumn. Be sure to watch out for kingfishers darting over the surface of the river.

Make your way over the Kelvin, doubling back on yourself through the trees that line the opposite bank. Cross the bright green lawns to then continue on the high path until you meet a road that leads through the complex of Glasgow University's Vet School. Around here, you'll find a lot of exotic plants that are a spectacle of colour in spring.

Go up the road in the same direction to a gate where you turn left along the minor Ilay Road for a short time before slipping through a large entrance on your left into Dawsholm Park proper, part of the Garscube Estate which was bought by the Glasgow Corporation in 1922 and has

been left in a natural state to the delight of birdwatchers and wildlife lovers. At a crossroads, choose the widest central path. After cresting its slight brae, an avenue stretches downhill before you with a barrier at the end.

Head down here to come out on a wide open space of former blaze pitches. Continue along the main estate road, which you'll find popular with dog walkers, all the way back to Dalsholm Road, turning right to return to the station.

◀ The Lady Campbell Bridge over the River Kelvin

This chapter covers the rugged upland region stretching west and southwest of the city of Glasgow, featuring the county of Inverclyde which occupies the coastal strip along the south bank of the Firth of Clyde and the sprawling county of Renfrewshire that surrounds it.

Here you will find the high, desolate moorland of the Renfrewshire Heights, a paradise for the solitary walker, as well as sparkling lochs, wooded glens and easily surmounted little hills that give fantastic outlooks across the Firth of Clyde to Bute and Arran.

Much of this area is occupied by Clyde Muirshiel, a windswept expanse of hill country that tumbles down to the Ayrshire coast and forms Scotland's biggest regional park. In the northwestern reaches of the park, one level route follows the historic aqueduct of the Greenock Cut, passing Loch Thom and giving views down to Inverkip. Further

inland, a lovely walk explores the Locherwood Community Woodland and Ladymuir Reservoir, taking in panoramic views from a hilltop detour. At Lochwinnoch, you can stroll round the popular loch at Castle Semple and explore stunning bluebell woods.

This chapter also contains some classic wee hill routes. East of Loch Thom above Greenock, an exhilarating circuit climbs Corlick Hill before crossing the Gryfe Reservoirs. From Neilston, south of Paisley, there's a choice of two routes up small hills with tons of character – Duncarnock, with its Neolithic hill fort, and the distinctive flat-topped Neilston Pad just down the road.

Near busy Paisley, you can also find great city views following the Tannahill Walkway in the Gleniffer Braes Country Park and closer to the city is a stroll along the Clyde and under the Erskine Bridge to enjoy Boden Boo plantation.

Snypes Dam from the top of Neilston Pad ▶

Inverclyde and Renfrewshire

Erskine Bridge and the Boden Boo

Distance **3km** Time **1 hour 30**
Terrain **tarmac waterside walkway, then good gravel and dirt tracks (can be muddy) with one fairly steep but short stretch** Access **buses (23, 23A) from Glasgow Renfield Street and Central Station to Bridgewater Shopping Centre**

Stroll along the banks of the historic River Clyde, once Glasgow's vital trade link to the outside world, from Erskine. The walk detours to a little beach before climbing underneath the Erskine Bridge and wandering through the trees and flowers of Boden Boo plantation.

An easy waterfront walk to enjoy a close-up of Erskine Bridge, this route should be accessible for most people and it includes only one short climb on a gravel track under the bridge. Start on the south bank of the River Clyde just a short

walk from Erskine Swimming Pool and Bridgewater Shopping Centre on Kilpatrick Drive. You'll see a car park on the right here, where you should head out to the waterside and turn left onto the wide tarmac Erskine Riverfront Walkway.

In front of you is the Erskine Bridge, the most downstream of all the Clyde bridges, which links the M8 motorway with the A82 to Loch Lomond and beyond. Above it on the north side of the river are the Kilpatrick Hills which stretch from the Vale of Leven to Strathblane.

Shortly after passing the stark Erskine Bridge Hotel, the walkway crosses a little bridge and goes right. Turn right at the next junction, signposted Erskine Bridge and Boden Boo: this intriguing-sounding spot is a pretty plantation on slightly higher ground.

There is a brief amble through greenery,

still on an excellent path, before it crosses another bridge to rejoin the riverside. You have bypassed Erskine Harbour here to come out on Old Ferry Road: cross this and the car park opposite to enter a wide green community space, once part of the sprawling estate of Erskine House and now a perfect place for dog walkers and families.

Here, a signpost directs you to Erskine Beach and Boden Boo woodland. It's worth taking a few minutes to visit the beach, which is accessed by a small trail off to the right. From the beach, you can continue towards the bridge and pick up a trail back onto the main route or simply return up the small trail. The main route heads straight through the park until you are standing almost directly beneath the Erskine Bridge. Here, there's a fork: take the gravel track on the left for an abrupt climb under the bridge, passing two of the bridge piers, weaving your way under the structure and levelling off.

The path then dips down through the Boden Boo woodland plantation. On a sunny day, this is a great, secluded spot to catch some rays among the tall grass and pretty flowers, and there are some lovely large mature trees here. The main path winds in roughly the same direction to

emerge further up Old Ferry Road. Turn left to access an excellent tarmac path on the right after around 100m. At the next junction, take a left towards Erskine Harbour and riverside, following the next sign for the walkway. You're now on familiar ground as you follow the walkway all the way back to the start, this time enjoying the views upstream to Glasgow.

◀ Erskine Beach

25

The Gryfe and Corlick Hill

Distance 9.5km Time 2 hours
Terrain public and forestry roads, rough
tracks; easy ground but with several
gates Map OS Explorer 341
Access no regular bus service, but from
Drumfrochar Station in Greenock it is
3km up the steep Old Largs Road (no
pavement) to Gryfe Reservoir

A journey into the less-known
countryside of Inverclyde, taking in the
small but perfectly formed Corlick Hill
and its fabulous airy views before
crossing the Gryfe Reservoir system.

This walk starts above Greenock at
a parking area by the Old Largs Road
between the Gryfe Reservoirs and Loch
Thom. Driving from Greenock town
centre, take the A78 Inverkip Road,
making a sharp left at a sign for Old Largs
Road after a long uphill. The parking area
is about 3km along this road by a stone
bridge and cattle grid. Turn right to walk
gently uphill on the road you approached

by for around 2km. Despite being the
main road in this area, there's a sense of
space here, with big sky above and high,
windswept moorland all around. In fact,
you might spot a few paraponters
launching themselves off nearby hills, as
well as the local model airplane club's
launch pad, a patch of immaculate grass,
by the roadside.

Take the second road on the right
(not the one for Darndaff): this rises
gradually over the moorland with
glimpses of Arrochar, Loch Fyne and Holy
Loch. When the road starts to climb left,
near a telephone mast just after Whitelees
Cottage, leave it to continue eastwards by
a track signposted for Corlick Hill. At the
foot of the hill, leave this track to drop
down over grass, cross a burn and follow
a broken-down stone wall to a stile. From
here, there's an obvious desire line
straight up the hill which gives a stiff
10-minute workout.

From the top, you'll see the Firth of

◄ The Gryfe Reservoir

Clyde and the panorama of the northern peaks on one side, but there are also great views in every other direction – over Renfrewshire and across the rolling hills of Inverclyde and Ayrshire to Arran.

Drop back down to the track, retracing your steps along this for about 30m before crossing a large gate on your left to descend by an old farm track.

Go left at a fork to pass an old shieling and copse of trees. Continue on the track, climbing over a gate and skirting around another copse to head downhill towards the reservoir and the bottom left corner of a field, where there are several gates. Climb the gate straight ahead to keep two fences on your right, and follow these downhill to a gate at the bottom of a second field. Beyond this gate, turn right to follow a grassy embankment all the way across the reservoir system.

Heading over the top of Gryfe Reservoir Number 1 with Number 2 below gives the feeling of walking on water. The track leads over a small bridge to meet a gate onto a bumpy forestry road. Turn right for a pleasant walk alongside the reservoir and, when you reach a junction, go right to return to the Old Largs Road at the start.

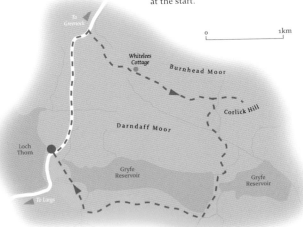

Greenock Cut and Shielhill Glen

**Distance 11km Time 2 hours 30
Terrain good roads and gravel paths with
some later muddy sections Access no
direct bus service, but train from
Glasgow Central to Drumfrochar Station
in Greenock (1km from Overton on route)**

Join an historic aqueduct for a long
but easy journey through a varied
landscape that switches from moorland
to wooded gorge with easy navigation
and great views.

Start at Cornalees Bridge Visitor Centre
which is part of Clyde Muirshiel Regional
Park and located by Loch Thom, south
of Greenock, off the A78 Greenock to
Inverkip road. There is no direct bus
service to Cornalees, but you can catch
a train from Glasgow to Drumfrochar
Station and walk to Overton, starting
the route at its midway point.

From the visitor centre car park, take
the northbound road beyond the
fisherman's hut and a compensation
reservoir on your right before passing
Loch Thom Cottage, the weir system and
the Loch Thom reservoir itself. For such
an accessible area, this is surprisingly
peaceful and within minutes you are into
an area of remote moorland and still
waters. The track continues on a rising
NNE course, past a well built by the
Argyll and Sutherland Highlanders in
the early 20th century, with views
starting to appear at the highest point
after about 2.5km.

Ignore any turnings to the left and
instead wind steadily downhill past a
couple of smaller reservoirs towards
Overton and the old water engineer's
cottage. There, go through the gate to
bear left along the gravel path that
follows a mini-canal – the Cut itself.

This impressive piece of engineering

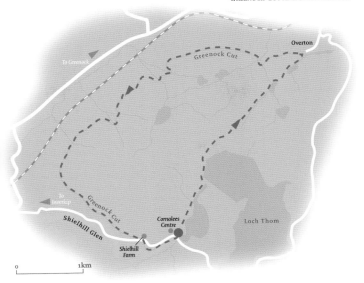

was created by Robert Thom in 1825. The aqueduct channelled water from the Great Reservoir, now named Loch Thom, in a clockwise direction, providing drinking water for the people of Greenock and hydro-power for its factories, which included a paper mill and sugar refinery. The Cut was designated an Ancient Monument in 1972 and there are many old weirs, bridges, work huts and outflows visible around it. The water in the Cut still flows, but is drunk no longer.

Follow the gravel track as it veers round to give a great view of the Firth of Clyde with Helensburgh across the water and an unexpectedly close Greenock just below. Bright green fields and patches of forestry soon take the place of houses on the nearby braes, with the familiar tower of Inverkip's old power station visible, as well as the countless yachts in its marina.

Around 2km before the end, the Cut skirts the top of Shielhill Glen, an area designated a Site of Special Scientific Interest (SSSI) for its rich mix of old deciduous woodland, before meeting the road at Shielhill Farm. Go directly across the road and through a pair of iron gates to follow the Cut on its last leg back to the visitor centre – skirting above the tumbling waters of a gorge and a delightful waterfall before the end.

◀ Looking towards Inverkip from the Greenock Cut

Locherwood and Windy Hill

Distance **12km** Time **3 hours**
Terrain **forestry roads and paths, but
fainter trails can get muddy; rough
heather on Windy Hill** Map **OS Explorer
341** Access **train from Glasgow Central
to Lochwinnoch (5km away); SPT's
Ring'n'Ride Gryffe Valley bus service
(965) can arrange drop-offs and pick-ups
at Barnbrock Farm**

**This circuit of trails through grassland,
woodland and moor is rich in plant and
insect life and you may even spot a roe
deer or two. It's well worth venturing
out to Windy Hill, with its fine views across
the Clyde Valley, up to the Arrochar Alps
and down to the Galloway Hills.**

Start at the Locherwood Community
Woodland car park opposite Barnbrock
Farm: you'll find this on the edge of Clyde
Muirshiel Regional Park off the B786
Kilmacolm to Lochwinnoch road. From
the car park, an obvious estate road
meanders past young oak and rowan to a
fork just beyond a large stone house.
Go right here onto a grassy path which
rises gradually around the forest. When
it splits, carry on uphill (left) to head high
over grassland with widening views over
Glasgow to Ben Lomond.

As the path starts to make a winding
descent, there's a fork. Go left, indicated
by a blue arrow, to cross a wee wooden
bridge, the first of many. The path now
keeps company with a stane dyke, leaving
it to turn right into trees where you'll find
a display board with map. After crossing
a wooden bridge, turn right to follow the
burn upstream, persevering even when
the path diminishes to a faint boggy trail.
Cross another bridge and continue
upstream on the opposite bank, taking
care over the broken pallets that have
been positioned to help walkers cross
the wettest patches.

Ignoring the next bridge you see, in a hollow on your right, carry straight on along the higher path to wind through several clearings and cross a bridge ahead. The path fades in places as it climbs past a hide, through a large clearing and over a small bridge in a landscape filled with flowers, mosses and grasses in summer. When you come to a crossroads of faint trails and a display board, follow the red arrow to climb Windy Hill.

Cross a stone wall by a stile and turn left towards Windy Hill with its visible cairn (not to be confused with the craggy hill on the right). The track all but disappears, but keep close to the wall as you tackle this rough terrain. Ignore a gate at the end of the wall and continue over heather, roughly following a fenceline to a meeting of fences after a copse of trees. Here, a stile gives access to Windy Hill which, as the name suggests, catches a good breeze!

From the top, the 360-degree views are superb – north to Ben Lomond, the Arrochar Alps and Argyll and south to Tinto in Lanarkshire and the Galloway Hills. Retrace your steps to the crossroads in the clearing, where you should turn left

to eventually reach a forestry road. Follow this until you find yourself standing under a pylon line, turning right towards Ladymuir Reservoir where a waterside track takes you past a dazzling array of wildflowers and insects in summer. At the foot of the reservoir, take the path that runs parallel with the pylons away from the water.

After crossing a stile, the path undulates gently over grassland. Turn left towards the city just beyond a picnic bench and, at the next fork, make a sharp left to go downhill and cross through a broken section of wall after 30m or so. Continue through newly-planted trees and over a wonky-looking wooden sleeper bridge before soon crossing the burn again via a big stone slab.

Follow the path as it rises and levels off and when you meet the estate road of your outward journey, turn left and then contour right to return to the car park.

◄ Looking north to the Ladymuir Plantation

Castle Semple and Parkhill Wood

Distance **7km** Time **2 hours** Terrain **cycle tracks to start and woodland paths that can get muddy** Access **train from Glasgow Central to Lochwinnoch (1.5km away)**

This is an easygoing walk for any time of year, but it really shouldn't be missed in the springtime when Parkhill Wood is a carpet of bluebells. Park Hill itself is just 90m high, but gives views across Lochwinnoch and the hills beyond.

Castle Semple Visitor Centre in Lochwinnoch is part of Clyde Muirshiel Regional Park and offers watersports and other outdoor activities, including boat and bike hire. There is also an RSPB nature reserve and visitor centre – complete with hides and birdwatching areas – near the train station, a great alternative start point that links with

Castle Semple Visitor Centre by a lochside track (adding around 3km to the walk in total).

Despite being well-equipped for activity hunters, this area also has a lot to offer the solitary walker looking for some peace and quiet. The views across Castle Semple Loch and beyond are lovely, while Parkhill Wood is renowned for its flowers.

From the visitor centre, follow the shore on a good gravel track to a fork at a lifebuoy after about 10 minutes. Branch right onto a cycle track, signposted for Glasgow, which leads down a tree-lined avenue. Just after the view opens up over the water, you will see an old church, signposted, on your left. Come off the track to access the church by a gate.

Founded in 1504 by the First Lord Semple and now in the care of Historic Scotland, the Collegiate Church was intended as a place of learning as well as worship and came to be considered one of the finest of its kind in the country. Sadly, Lord Semple was killed at the Battle of Flodden in 1513 and his body returned to

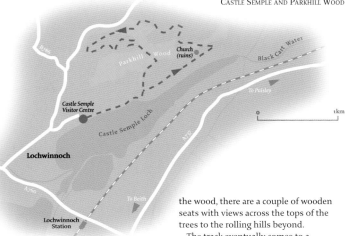

be entombed in the ornate eastern extension. The church fell out of use after the Reformation, but continued as a burial enclosure for a long time.

Exiting the church, turn left onto the path, and continue past rhododendron bushes to a fork near the top of the hill. Follow the most obvious route (right) through a gate into Parkhill Wood, ignoring the fainter track running alongside the wood. In bluebell season, you will see the first significant patches here as you head steadily downhill. After passing through a gateway, leave the track to follow a path waymarked with a yellow arrow to the right. You can forget about route finding for a while and enjoy the path as it meanders through glades that in late spring are a sea of blue. As you approach the highest point on the edge of

the wood, there are a couple of wooden seats with views across the tops of the trees to the rolling hills beyond.

The track eventually comes to a junction with yellow arrows pointing in both directions. The fainter of the tracks (right) leads up Park Hill itself, joining a fence for the ascent to the top where you can enjoy the open space and views across the loch and beyond. The bluebells are probably at their best on the slopes here, where their heavy perfume can be almost overwhelming.

From the top, continue by the track as it drops down the other side of the hill and rejoins the main woodland path. Among the features it passes is a pond overlooked by a small stone dwelling which was built with curved corners at the rear so that evil spirits would not malinger. After crossing a little wooden bridge, turn right to follow a white arrow out of Parkhill Wood, back across the cycle track and down to Castle Semple Loch. Return along the shore to the centre.

Tannahill Walkway over Gleniffer Braes

Distance 8km **Time** 2 hours 30
Terrain good tarmac paths and woodland
trails, some open ground for which
walking boots are recommended; steps
and stiles **Access** train from Glasgow
Central to Paisley Canal Station; buses
(1, 4, 166) from Paisley to Caplethill Road
near the end of Glenfield Road

**A rewarding walk in a rugged upland
Renfrewshire country park with one of
the best viewpoints across Glasgow
and the Clyde Valley.**

Start at Gleniffer Braes Country Park
information centre at Glen Park, located
just off Glenfield Road in Paisley. Here, at
the back of the car park, you'll find a
nature trail heading uphill to converge
with the main path, the Tannahill
Walkway, after just a few minutes. Named
after Paisley weaver poet and songwriter
Robert Tannahill, the walkway passes
through a glen with an interesting
cultural history. As a natural

amphitheatre, it became a venue for open-
air choral concerts, attracting tens of
thousands of people to the surrounding
slopes. The first concert was held in 1874
to mark the centenary of Tannahill's birth.

Ignore the sign for Brownside and
Fereneze Braes and carry straight on
uphill by the main track, resisting any
temptation to branch right as you keep to
the higher path to enter dense woodland
and climb steps with a wooden handrail.
A short signposted diversion to the
bottom of the secretive waterfall of
Craigie Linn is worth the 10-minute
detour, before returning to the main
route. At a fork just after a small burn,
follow the lower track signposted for
Robertson Park to meet a road. Cross this
and go through the metal gate on the
opposite side of the car park for
increasingly good views across open
ground grazed by Highland cattle. This
excellent path makes a quick ascent
alongside Gleniffer Gorge, past the old

◀ Summer flowers on Gleniffer Braes

bridge, which is now dangerous and fenced-off, to another bridge which takes you safely across.

Pick up the trail heading downhill on the right towards Paisley to soon rejoin the main walkway, with dramatic views across Greater Glasgow to the hills in the north and the west. Carry on to Robertson Park, which is an excellent panoramic viewpoint. A playpark here will entertain younger children.

The second half of the walk crosses rougher ground, but there shouldn't be any route-finding difficulties. Pass through a gate just above the playpark to head diagonally across tussocky grassland until you pick up a rough track which soon meets the Tannahill Walkway. Instead of returning on the walkway, take the high track across a field and follow the line of the fence and trees which mark the boundary of the course at Paisley Golf Club. As you cross open ground, head for the flagpole, which brings you out neatly at the golf club car park.

Cross the car park and a stile directly ahead, maintaining this course to pass through a copse of trees and pick up a very old and somewhat muddy road. A standing stone east of this track makes for an interesting little diversion. Follow the track downhill to access a better road through a gate and follow this briefly before it bends away at the edge of the woodland. Re-enter the woods at this corner to join a trail heading downhill to the right. Descend by this to return to the walkway and car park.

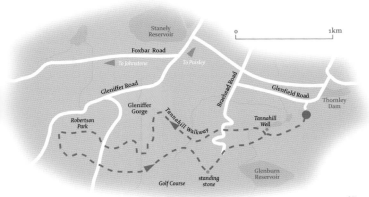

Duncarnock and Glanderston Dam

Distance 2km (+3km each way if walking
to start) **Time** 1 hour 30 (+1 hour 30 if
walking out from Neilston) **Terrain** some
rough ground and several stiles; gentle
ascent with one final short steep pull
Access train from Glasgow Central to
Neilston, 3km from start

A quick and entertaining ascent up
a volcanic plug known locally as the
Craigie, also the site of a hillfort in
Neolithic times. The route crosses a
varied landscape of green pastures and
open hill before returning around
Glanderston Dam reservoir.

Duncarnock sits 3km southeast of
Neilston, surrounded by rolling farmland
with views across Greater Glasgow to Ben
Lomond. To approach from Neilston
Station, head out onto Kingston Road

and turn right towards Stewarton, then
left along Kirkton Road at Neilston
Bowling Club. Follow this winding minor
road (no pavement) for just over 2.5km,
turning left at a T-junction and then next
right to reach a small parking area on a
bend in the road at the top of a farm track.

Go through a gate and walk along
the farm track for 300m, crossing two
fences on the right here to access the
reservoir embankment. Turn left along
the bank to pass an old irrigation channel
and step over a low wire fence to continue
alongside the water. Duncarnock appears
clearly before you at this point, a lovely-
looking hill with plenty of character.

On meeting an outflow at the far end,
use the stile and little wooden bridge on

your left to cross, then continue through farmland alongside a line of trees, contouring around the reservoir towards a drystane dyke topped with a fence. The climb over this is made easy by some long pieces of wood and straddling boulders.

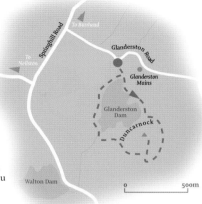

The adventurous might now take a direct line up the hill to make a circuit, but this track is steep and potentially slippery. The easiest route follows a worn path to the left, winding away from the reservoir parallel to the drystane wall, around the base of Duncarnock. As you come to the back of the hill, there's another steep ascent option but the easiest approach is to continue by this nice and gentle ascending path.

Finally, a short climb of around 30m at a fair gradient takes you onto the little ridge behind the fort. Turn right along the ridge for the trig point and views over Glasgow, the rolling green fields that surround it and the hills beyond. It's easy to see features in this hill that would have made it a good choice for a fort: the top is almost bowl-shaped, providing good shelter and corralling for livestock.

There are big rewards for this short walk. The views are quite wonderful and it's a peaceful spot to bring a family for a picnic, although this is an ancient monument so great care should be taken

not only with access but also in keeping it clean and litter-free.

There are a number of different ways off the hill, all steeper, some of them considerably so. The most accessible alternative would be by the path heading straight up the hill from the drystane dyke. However, all but the most sure-footed can expect to come down any alternative routes on their bums, especially after rain: the best route down is the way you came up.

At the bottom, you can return the way you came or continue around Glanderston Dam without too much difficulty to get back to the start.

◀ The summit of Duncarnock

Neilston Pad and Craighall Dam

Distance 4km Time 1 hour Terrain mostly good ground but can get muddy in places; some stiles and kissing gates with a short climb to the top Access train from Glasgow Central to Neilston, 1km from the Pad

A quiet and easy loop around a landmark flat-topped hill with far-reaching views.

With its easy paths, green spaces and great views, Neilston Pad is a great favourite with local families. The route starts around 2km southwest of Neilston off the Neilston to Stewarton road.

If arriving by car, turn off this road at the signs for Harelaw Farm and Harelaw Trout Fishery and park in the larger car park next to the water pump station. If approaching from Neilston on foot,

however, you can turn off the Stewarton road just after leaving town, where you see the countryside access signs, to join the route further round.

Go through a kissing gate at the back of the parking area, where a good hard-packed path leads you northwards to a crossroads after about 500m. Both main options encircle the Pad, but if you want to take in the top of the Pad first then take the smaller third path marked by a post. This gives a straightforward and fairly gentle climb through young pine forest to reach more open ground with good views towards Glasgow and over green rolling hills.

At a mature section of forestry, the path crosses a stile and continues by the fenceline to the diminutive cairn at the

◀ Neilston Pad

top of the Pad. Although in itself the top is fairly featureless, the views stretch extensively from the Campsies to the Trossachs, Arrochar and down over Renfrewshire, Ayrshire and even on a good day to Arran.

There are a number of faint paths enabling those familiar with the Pad to find different ways up and down. However, these are less apparent during the summer when there has been a lot of growth, so if it's your first visit it's best to retrace your steps for the first part of the descent. About 10m beyond the stile that you encountered on your way up, turn left onto a path which takes a pleasant diagonal line down the side of the Pad with good open views. When this splits at a small post, turn right to rejoin the main hard-packed track that goes all the way round the Pad.

Heading left, this soon passes through a kissing gate and bears broadly north past sheep pens. A large farm will appear ahead on the right, but you should bear left at the first main fork in the track, passing through several kissing gates

as you wind beneath the Pad.

The route also skirts the Craighall Dam reservoir, where you might want to sit and enjoy the peace as you are now just a short distance from the start. The track carries on easily round the Pad without too much gradient and, when it meets another track, you are back at the start of the loop. Head right to return to the car park.

Map labels: To Neilston · Barr Hill · Snypes Dam · Neilston Pad · Craighall Dam · To Stewarton · Harelaw Dam · 0 500m

Immortalised in song, story and poem, Loch Lomond holds a special place in the hearts of many Glaswegians, who regard it as their very own city treasure.

These walks give some very different perspectives over the loch – one starts in Balloch Castle Country Park to discover a secret viewpoint. To the northeast, by Gartocharn, you can get a stunning panorama of the loch with a quick pilgrimage up tiny Duncryne. In contrast, Beinn Dubh, above Luss on the western shore, gives a fantastic workout for anyone building up to the munros, as well as a great view of Ben Lomond.

Three routes start by Balmaha on the quieter eastern shore: one follows part of the West Highland Way to take in Conic Hill right on the Highland Boundary Fault; a series of waymarked trails wander up the gentle wooded slopes of Cashel Forest; and an easy circuit calls in at an unspoilt beach and hilltop viewpoint on the island of Inchcailloch.

Much nearer to Glasgow, but offering far-reaching views to Loch Lomond and the mountains beyond, lie the Kilpatrick Hills, strung out to the north of the River Clyde between Strathblane and Dumbarton. Chief among the attractions of this hill range is the unusual geological feature of the Whangie, accessed from the Queen's View with its outlook to Loch Lomond. More interesting geology can be explored on a walk above Old Kilpatrick and the natural terraces known as the Slacks, with open views back over the Clyde to Glasgow and the Erskine Bridge.

A final route goes 'doon the watter' with a visit to Charles Rennie Mackintosh's splendid Hill House and the woodland up behind Helensburgh.

The Kilpatrick Hills, Loch Lomondside and Helensburgh

Cochno Hill and Jaw Reservoir

Distance 9km (+2km each way if walking
to start) **Time** 2 hours 30 (+30 minutes
each way if walking to start)
Terrain fields and hill trails which can get
muddy, and roads to start and finish
Map OS Explorer 347 **Access** bus (17) from
Hope Street to Cochno Road, Hardgate

Easily accessible from the west of the
city, the Kilpatricks are great wee hills
with lots of character. This route heads
up through farmland to reach remote
reservoirs and broad hilltops with
excellent views over the city below.

Begin the walk at the big car park near
Cochno Farm, reached by taking the A8014
turn-off to Hardgate/Duntocher at the
Clydebank roundabout and then going
left at Hardgate roundabout and right up
Cochno Brae. Regular buses go along
Cochno Road.

On leaving the car park, follow the sign
for the access path. After about 100m,
another sign directs you off the road and

into the fields as you begin to head up
towards the hills.

Keeping your distance from any
livestock which may be around, follow the
fenceline to reach a farm road. When this
comes to a junction, cross the stile in
front of you – green arrows on posts mark
the way – into another field and aim for
the trees. Follow the fenceline as it bends
round to the top of this field and head left
through a break in the trees to reach the
open hillside.

The rewarding sight of the Grey Mare's
Tail waterfall soon appears on your right
as you follow the rumbling burn up the
hillside to Jaw Reservoir and some
excellent views back over the city.

Turning west at the reservoir, pick up
the trail once again as it rises above the
water and meanders along a wide area of
open moorland. The broad summit will
appear before you after the reservoir has
disappeared from view behind, and there
are a network of paths just before the
final ascent. Although the highest point

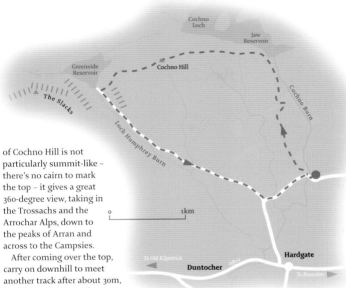

of Cochno Hill is not particularly summit-like – there's no cairn to mark the top – it gives a great 360-degree view, taking in the Trossachs and the Arrochar Alps, down to the peaks of Arran and across to the Campsies.

After coming over the top, carry on downhill to meet another track after about 30m, heading roughly southwest and continuing on level ground before dipping down towards Greenside Reservoir with the distinctive hillside feature of the Slacks above it.

The track follows an undulating course, passing under two power lines where, in a dip directly beneath the second, it splits. Take the path on the right to wind your way towards the reservoir, descending quite suddenly at the end to emerge on a gravel road at the water's edge. Follow this road, which shadows Loch Humphrey Burn all the way to the bottom of the hill,

passing a couple of ruined buildings as you leave the hillside behind.

Carry on past a farm on your right and, a little further on, the imposing concrete tower at the old water treatment works.

You will soon join up with the road which you took to get to the car park at the start. Follow the green arrow for Cochno Farm if you need to return to the car park or carry on downhill to catch your bus back to Glasgow.

◄ From the slopes of Cochno Hill

Loch Humphrey and the Slacks

Distance 9km **Time** 3 hours **Terrain** some tarmac, but mostly off-path over open ground and through rough heather and bracken **Map** OS Explorer 347 **Access** train from Glasgow to Old Kilpatrick

A circular walk over the grassy heather-clad slopes above the Slacks, a hillside of natural terraces in the Kilpatricks.

From Old Kilpatrick Station, go up Station Road and continue straight on after passing under the A82 roadbridge to reach the Old Kilpatrick Gasworks. Follow the road round and turn right at a junction, going through a signposted gate. This road leads past a house and small ruined shed before crossing a cattle grid by another 'Loch Humphrey' sign.

At a fork, branch right onto the rougher track, stopping just before a burn when you are almost in line with the farmhouse below. From here, a very faint trail takes you onto the higher ground to your right,

passing a boxed-off tree as you climb gradually northeast.

Soon the path becomes more distinct. Wherever it splits, stick to the higher most direct ascent until you emerge on a grassy track which takes a long, diagonal line along the side of the hill.

As you come up to the top of this hill, the track forks: turn right for a stretch awash with ferns in summer. On a good day, as you gain height, you can see as far south as Ailsa Craig in the Firth of Clyde.

The path continues to climb as it bears right, and goes through a broken-down drystane dyke, then heads up a little rocky outcrop, coming out onto a heather-clad prow. Head roughly north away from the Clyde – there is no longer any real track but as you continue straight up over open moor, there's a drystane dyke on your left. Maintain this course after passing the corner of the dyke until the gradient levels off and you can see the trig point in

◄ On the Kilpatrick Braes

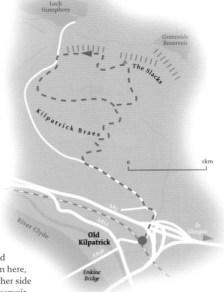

the northeast, then head for this. The going will be easier if you can pick up a small track which leads over a few heather banks and through a wire fence. From the trig point, you can see Greenside Reservoir and Cochno Hill to the right, while the other Kilpatrick Hills including Duncolm are ahead of you.

After admiring the view, head west by a grassy path. When you find yourself in a dip, take a path on the right to descend fairly sharply into a hollow. Don't follow the track straight down to a fence when it forks; instead take the gentler option round to the right to pass the end of the fence. After crossing a burn here, you'll pick up the track on the other side with a nice view of Greenside Reservoir.

The path climbs up along the top of a widening ridge, accompanying the fenceline westwards. At the end of the fence, drop down in the same direction over open ground to join the Loch Humphrey and Berry Bank access road. After a short on-road descent, turn left onto a track by the corner of a fence, crossing a little platform over a burn. Don't go straight uphill, but instead take the lower track to the right, running parallel to the road.

Carry on walking on the main path after passing through a broken drystane dyke,

roughly parallel with a stone wall on your left. The path becomes very faint, but hold your course, until you meet another track. Turn right onto this to drop through a dell, heading in the direction of Erskine Bridge as the views open up below.

This takes you out onto the track you were on earlier in the walk. Descend the long, diagonal grassy stretch, through the trees and gate and back onto the hillside above the farmhouse. Return to the road and the start.

The Doughnut and Lang Craigs

Distance 7km (+2km each way if walking to start) **Time** 2 hours (+30 minutes each way if starting from Milton) **Terrain** fields and hill trails (can get muddy) with a high and exposed return by Lang Craigs and a steep descent to finish
Map OS Explorer 347 **Access** bus (75) from Hope Street to Milton; Overtoun House is a 2km walk away up Milton Brae from the A82

A moderately challenging walk over rolling moorland from Overtoun House above Milton, Dumbarton, to Doughnot Hill for rewarding views up to Loch Lomond. The optional return along the top of Lang Craigs also gives great views but is quite exposed.

Overtoun House, a 19th-century Scots baronial mansion, is reached by turning up Milton Brae from the A82.

From the car park just before you come to the house itself, take the first path that splits off the road on the right and follow this gently uphill, keeping right, to a metal fence at the edge of open moorland. Climb over this and pick up the path which heads roughly towards a small hill sitting out from the end of the crags. The path is faint at times but leads all the way around this small hill until the Doughnut – as it's known locally – comes into view.

As the track rises and approaches forestry, two stone slabs embedded in the path indicate where you should go left to climb the hill. After an initial descent, strike directly northeast up the slopes to reach the summit. There are no paths as such and it's fairly rough underfoot, but you'll be at the top in no time.

On reaching the cairn, you can often

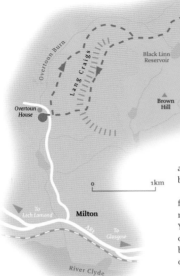

enjoy clear views of Loch Lomond and the Arrochar Alps, as well as the rest of the Kilpatricks and the Campsies, while the views down over Dumbarton, the Clyde and further to the south and west are also excellent.

Although many people do this hill as an out-and-back, you can make a circuit of it by returning along the top of the crags you walked under on your outward journey.

Returning to the path you left to tackle the Doughnut, follow the desire line up on to the top of Lang Craigs and along the edge of the trees.

Not long after the terrain levels off, the track – which has become quite clear now – stops just before a section where the side of the hill has fallen away. Simply step over the fence here to avoid any danger and continue following the track. Taking care not to stray too near to the edge, enjoy the high views and settle in to rambling along here for at least another 1.5km before descending.

To find the way down, look for a flattened part of the fence with a path nearby leading off the side of the hill. You should have just passed a junction of drystane walls beneath the crags and be looking directly down on the corner of Overtoun House.

After coming through the fence, pick up the path which leads sharply down through a small rocky passage – the rock is like cut steps but can be tricky if wet – before heading directly downhill.

The path then winds its way down through ferns and under trees before coming to a halt at a fence on flatter ground. Cross it where you can and continue straight down in the direction of the road to Overtoun House. The path fades here, but just strike out across the fields – the ground is rough again – towards the car park, crossing one last metal fence on the way back to the start by Overtoun House.

◀ Looking up to the Doughnut

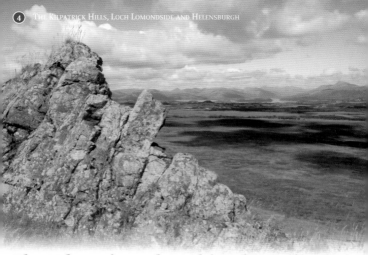

The Whangie and Auchineden Hill

Distance 4km **Time** 1 hour 30
Terrain steep start; rough paths with
boggy sections, particularly on
Auchineden Hill **Map** OS Explorer 347
Access bus (8) from Buchanan Street Bus
Station to Drymen (request stop)

An airy walk starting from the Queen's
View, where Queen Victoria had her first
glimpse of Loch Lomond in 1879, to the
Whangie, an atmospheric geological
fault, and the high point of Auchineden
Hill with its views over the Kilpatrick
Hills, Loch Lomondside and Campsies.

Start at the Queen's View car park on the
A809 between Milngavie and Drymen.
Plenty of people come here solely to make
the 10-minute walk from the car park to
the viewpoint, which gives a brilliant

panorama across the Loch Lomond &
The Trossachs National Park.

From the back left corner of the car park,
go over a stile for a stretch of duckboards
and a brief but steep climb to the top of a
rocky outcrop. This hill is named the
Queen's View after Queen Victoria who
is said to have seen the bonnie banks of
Loch Lomond for the first time from here.

Continue westwards past an old stile on
the left, ignoring the option to climb the
hill here and instead traversing this and
the crags on a level but often muddy path
for around 1km. At a fork, go right along
the lower path, where a small forest
comes into view beneath you as you near
the Whangie. When you see the boulders
that mark the start of the Whangie
immediately in front of you, the path

◀ Looking over Stockie Muir

splits three ways. It's easy to take the wrong path and miss this dramatic hidden feature, so take care to choose the highest one on the left, which heads up a sharp incline and into the gash in the rock that is the Whangie itself.

In Scots, 'whang' means 'to slice' and, although geologists believe the 250m-long passageway set between 10m-high cliffs was created by glacial movement, there are a couple of more colourful explanations for 'wha whanged the Whangie' in which the Devil has a starring role. The first tells how the Devil was in hot pursuit of God, who outmanoeuvred him. As he tried to turn quickly, the Devil sliced his tail into the ground, splitting the rock and creating the Whangie. Another legend is that the Devil was heading over Auchineden Hill, either on his way to or from a pow-wow with a coven of witches, when he whipped his tail in delight.

As you emerge from the Whangie, the path dips slightly, then veers left and contours about 150m uphill in an 'S' shape. Don't follow the path heading straight off into the distance, but instead take the initially vague path that climbs immediately right. This path soon improves, leading you to the trig point at the top of Auchineden Hill.

The route home is straightforward but the path is indistinct at times and crosses quite boggy ground. Head northeast along the top of the hill before dropping steeply north to the left of a mobile phone mast beside a copse of trees and stone wall. When you come to the old stile you met on your outward journey, follow the path down to the right to find the Queen's View once more and the way back to the start.

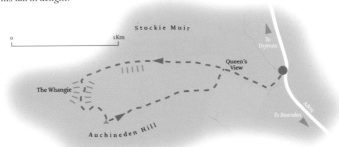

Whinney Hill from Balloch

Distance 10km Time **2 hours 45**
Terrain **walkways and good trails in the
country park with paths and steeper
ground on the hill** Map **OS Explorer 347**
Access **train from Glasgow Queen Street
to Balloch**

**A rewarding walk from Balloch, gateway
to the Loch Lomond & The Trossachs
National Park, to visit Balloch Castle
Country Park and a wonderful viewpoint
from Whinney Hill Wood.**

Balloch, at the southern tip of Loch
Lomond, makes for a great outing from
the city and is easily accessible by public
transport. For this longer walk, start at
the train station and turn right to follow
Balloch Road over the River Leven.

To enter Balloch Castle Country Park,
cross the large car park after the bridge
where you pick up a path at the back
into the Moss o' Balloch. After passing
a playpark, turn right onto a good
walkway and then left onto the main
park driveway, which is bordered by
majestic trees.

After a time, the woodland canopy
gives way to pristine lawns stretching
from the edge of the loch up to the castle,
with open views over the water to the
hills beyond – a lovely spot for a picnic.
The road splits into two above the lawns.
Stick to the lower one, which curls around
the castle.

Continue beyond the castle for about 10
minutes until you see a gravelled area on
your right where a sign marks the start of
a stony trail to the 250-acre Whinney Hill
Wood. This is rough underfoot with a fair
amount of ascent as it winds its way up

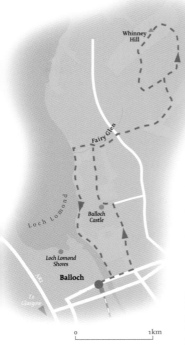

path meanders past young trees on the left and, in summer, swathes of foxgloves as well as orchids, buttercups and purple thistles. Enjoy the intermittent tree-framed views as the path steepens and runs alongside a stone wall for a short while. Where your route becomes less distinct (can be muddy), an acorn sign on a fence points the way to a better track.

Bear left to descend to a T-junction where you turn right for the start of your loop around Whinney Hill, soon coming to a gate. Take a left onto a stony track here: this fades after a kissing gate but an obvious desire line continues around the hill to arrive unexpectedly – and spectacularly – at the viewpoint, with its less-familiar Loch Lomond vista.

Carry on down the hill, with tantalising glimpses of the Campsies. The main track is reached just beyond another kissing gate: turn left onto this and then right uphill at the start of the loop to retrace your steps through the wood.

Back on tarmac in the park, keep an eye out for a trail on the right that takes you through Fairy Glen and onto the scenic Shore Walk. Follow this, with the loch on you right, keeping to the tracks nearest the water when there are other options. You'll find a small playground, walled gardens and ducks and swans to feed as the Shore Walk leads you along the banks of the River Leven to the start.

through this atmospheric ancient wood, close to a burn. Stick to the main path before turning left at a junction as the path steepens to climb into the thick of the wood, well above the burn. Eventually, this levels off to exit onto a road by a wooden gate. Cross the road to re-enter the wood by another gate.

The gradient eases as a hard-packed dirt

◄ From the top of Whinney Hill

The Secret of the Dumpling

Distance 2km **Time** 1 hour
Terrain on-road walking for approach
from Gartocharn; steep but short climb
on good path to top of hill **Access** train
from Glasgow Queen Street to Balloch;
buses (13, 313) from Balloch to Gartocharn

When you first encounter this hill and
its panoramic view across Loch Lomond,
it's like discovering your own Narnia.
There is a track to the top and the
summit is nice and flat – making it ideal
for a picnic – so be prepared to spend
longer on this friendly hill than it takes
to get up and down. The Dumpling is also
a great adventure for young children.

The tiny hill of Duncryne, a volcanic
plug known locally as the Dumpling, was
climbed nearly every day by the late
great Tom Weir, who lived in Gartocharn.
For fans of his television series, Weir's
Way, visiting the 142m Duncryne is a bit
of a pilgrimage. It's more of a mound than
a mountain but is ideally positioned for
great views and is a must-do, despite
being such a short outing.

Start from the village of Gartocharn on
the A811 Loch Lomond road. Turn off the
main road in the centre of the village,
heading away from the loch on a minor
road. Just after Duncryne House, you'll
come to a layby and kissing gate beside
the wood. Go through this, heeding the
signs about litter and that the wood is

off-limits as it has been 'reserved for teddy bears'!

Follow the well-worn path to make a gradual ascent and pass through another kissing gate at the edge of the wood. The path continues up a fenced-off walkway straight ahead. Accompany this up to and through yet another kissing gate, where the path forks. Take the right branch to climb steeply but surely up the south face of the hill.

It's a short ascent so there is plenty of time to stop and admire the views, which open up as you gain height. It might lack stature but Duncryne is not short on loveliness – and in no time at all you'll

have arrived at the trig point on top. The view from here is regarded as one of the best in central Scotland.

The return journey is purely a matter of retracing your steps, but take the time to linger on the wide and flat summit.

▼ On top of Duncryne

Enchanted Inchcailloch

Distance 3km **Time** 1 hour 30
Terrain steep in places, but with well-maintained woodland paths and steps
Access train from Glasgow Queen Street to Balloch and bus (309) from Balloch to Balmaha; ferry from Balmaha Boatyard

A nature-rich walk on the island of Inchcailloch on Loch Lomond, which takes in a wonderful viewpoint, a remote sandy bay and the ruins of an old kirkyard with links to St Kentigerna.

From the visitor centre in Balmaha, head down to the boatyard where, weather permitting, a ferry makes the trip across to Inchcailloch all year round. The five-minute jaunt across the sparkling waters of this famous loch elevate what is already a lovely little walk into a treasured outing.

On landing at the North Pier, a sign welcomes you to Loch Lomond National Nature Reserve, now in the care of Scottish Natural Heritage. As the island is valuable for its ancient woodlands and wetlands and the rich bird and plantlife they support, visitors should take care to preserve it. Inchcailloch – meaning Island of the Old Women – is also linked to St Kentigerna, who is said to have set up a community of nuns on the island and died here in 734AD.

From the jetty, head up the stone steps onto a good, gravel track which winds its way uphill. Intermittent duckboards and wooden steps make steeper sections much more accessible on this route. After about five minutes, you reach a crossroads and information board. The quickest way across the island is to

Descending by the northern path, the views open out briefly across the loch before you dive back into the trees for a winding descent to a T-junction. This time follow the sign for Port Bawn where an unspoilt sandy beach awaits.

To return, pick up the Low Path which heads past the toilets and over a wooden bridge to the right (ignore the path down to the jetty). As it begins to turn inland, the path is grassy and less defined though still excellent underfoot. Around 500m from Port Bawn, a post marked with a '5' on your left gives a short detour to the ruins of an old farm.

Return to the path and prepare for a long ascent by steps, after which you have two options: either take the track on the right or take the short detour to visit the church ruins and burial ground of the Clan MacGregor. Clan Chief Gregor MacGregor, cousin of the outlaw Rob Roy, is among those laid to rest here. There are no graves in the north part of the cemetery: according to local lore, that belongs to the Devil.

On leaving the burial ground, drop down some wooden steps to return to the Central Valley Path. Turn left at the next junction and follow the sign for the north jetty to get your boat back to Balmaha.

follow the sign for Port Bawn via the Central Valley Path. But it would be a crying shame to miss the breathtaking view from the highest point on the island, so instead cut left up the Summit Path.

This ducks under a thick canopy of tall oaks and alders with steps to aid progress up steep sections. As you emerge from the trees near the island's summit – the only viewpoint marked on the maps among all the islands of Loch Lomond – be prepared to be stunned. The view, with Conic Hill immediately to your right, Ben Lomond above it and the Arrochar Alps further up on the other side of the loch, is breathtaking.

◂ Inchcailloch from Balmaha Boatyard

Conic Hill from Balmaha

Distance 5km **Time** 2 hours **Terrain** steep
climb on woodland tracks and open hill
paths signposted as West Highland Way
on the way up **Map** OS Explorer 347
Access train from Glasgow Queen Street
to Balloch and bus (309) from Balloch
to Balmaha

**A grand hill ascent along part of the West
Highland Way, this circuit begins with a
short forest walk before heading up the
open hillside above Balmaha with
breathtaking views over Loch Lomond
and a pleasant return along the shore.**

Conic Hill is a great, short alternative to
Ben Lomond, with panoramic views over
Scotland's first national park to the Isle of
Arran in the southwest and the Southern

Highlands to the north. It also sits right
on the geological Highland Boundary
Fault and is a perfect introduction to the
area which is also a big draw for nature
lovers, with around 200 species of birds
and one quarter of Britain's wild plants
having been recorded here.

Start from the visitor centre in the
village of Balmaha on the eastern shore
of Loch Lomond, heading for the far
corner of the car park to access the Queen
Elizabeth Forest Park. You are on part of
the popular long-distance walking route,
the West Highland Way, and will be
following this for most of the ascent.

Initially, the route winds its way gently
along a pine forest track, following the
West Highland Way signpost left at a

◀ Climbing Conic Hill

junction before steepening. After passing through a gate, you break free of the forest canopy to begin the abrupt climb up rocky steps, with the open hillside giving increasingly good views – remember to turn around to enjoy them!

On reaching a plateau near the top of the bealach (hill pass), the track splits. This is a good place to stop and appreciate how much height you've gained. Keep to the more obvious path on the right to climb some rough stone steps out onto the shoulder of the hill, where stunning views open up to the north.

Continue uphill, still following the well-worn West Highland Way. After crossing a grassy patch where the route flattens out, a small stony path cuts into the hillside on your right. This marks the last push to the summit, and in no time you'll be standing on top of this wee mountain soaking up great views.

Retrace your steps downhill, following the main path back over the grassy patch to the prow of the hill. Instead of following the thistle left for Balmaha, carry straight on. The path initially seems to disappear, but shortly you will see a long, wide

ridge ahead. Drop down this lumpy ridge by a meandering grassy path – with spectacular views before you all the way – into a deciduous forest near the bottom.

When you meet the road, cross and go over a gate opposite towards the side of the loch. There is a nice beach here – a good place for a paddle if the weather allows! From here, a path takes you along the shore to the village. All too soon, you reach the small pier where you turn onto the road and walkway, passing a small marina before coming to the visitor centre at Balmaha. If you've worked up an appetite or thirst, the hospitable Oak Tree Inn is just across the road.

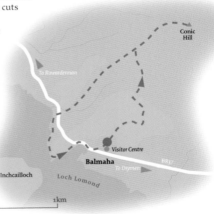

Cashel Forest Trails

Distance 6km **Time** 1 hour 30 (+30 mins for viewpoint detour) **Terrain** good landrover tracks and woodland trails; the slopes of this former hill farm are relatively gentle (total height gain 270m) **Access** train from Glasgow Queen Street to Balloch and bus (309) from Balloch to Balmaha, 4km from Cashel Farm

A gentler and less-known alternative to the nearby Conic Hill, with signposted woodland trails and some great options for shorter walks.

This area of ancient native woodland is being actively regenerated, creating an unusually diverse woodland environment which is home to a great variety of birds and flowers. While perhaps not as dramatic as neighbouring Conic Hill,

Cashel has its own special appeal and even in wet and overcast weather a walk here is always enjoyably atmospheric and entertaining.

Start at the old Cashel Farm on the eastern side of the loch, just north of Balmaha. For those wishing to use public transport, this can be reached from the village of Balmaha (where buses stop), 4km back along the road, via the famous long-distance walking trail, the West Highland Way. For most of this section, the trail follows the minor road, with a couple of pleasant deviations to the lochshore and into woodland.

From Cashel, pass the farm buildings to pick up your trail, heading uphill past the display board which shows a variety of trails for different ability levels.

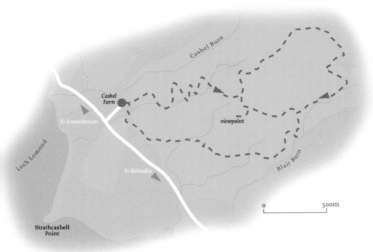

This route follows the longer green trail to its highest point, making use of the red trail on descent. As you follow the arrows uphill it does get quite steep, but the good landrover track makes easier work of this with rewarding views back over Loch Lomond.

Keep your eyes peeled for a post with a green arrow directing you off the main track to the right after you've climbed high above the glen. This is the start of the meandering route back down the hill, which remains good underfoot despite being a minor track.

Descend over softer ground to the sound of the rushing burn beneath you, passing young trees and bushes, before turning left at a T-junction to carry on along the main route. There's an option to detour to the right for views (add 30 minutes there and back). If doing so, leave the main track for a smaller path to the left after 1km or so: this leads to Cashel's main lookout point.

Return to the T-junction (you can also continue past the lookout to rejoin the main landrover track downhill to the start). The 2km return from the T-junction is a gradual, meandering descent on soft ground.

◀ Loch Lomond and Cashel Forest from Conic Hill

Beinn Dubh Horseshoe from Luss

Distance 11km **Time** 3 hours 30
Terrain grassy hillsides and dirt tracks,
peat hags at the summit; steep sections
of ascent and descent **Maps** OS Explorer
364 and 347 **Access** bus (916) from
Buchanan Street Bus Station or (305)
from Balloch to Luss

**Starting from the charming village of
Luss on the banks of Loch Lomond, this
high horseshoe is great practice for
anyone working up to the munros.**

Begin your hike from the pretty
conservation village of Luss on the
western shore of Loch Lomond. This was
the base for the popular Highland
television soap *Take the High Road*, which
ran for more than 20 years until 2001. Just
behind The Village Shop on the square,
cross the road and almost immediately
turn right, following the sign for Glen
Luss. Pass a primary school and climb
steps to the pedestrian bridge over the
busy A82, where Beinn Dubh can be seen
above right.

After crossing, go past a house on your
right and then pick up a stony path
straight ahead which goes through a
kissing gate and continues to the road
into Glen Luss. Ignore a signpost for a
quarry path pointing left here, instead
enter a large field by a metal gate on your
right. You are on the lower slopes of
Beinn Dubh here and will be climbing
roughly northwest up the long shoulder
of the hill to gain the top. A trail crosses
the field to a gate and stile higher up
where it gains definition as it heads
through a line of trees, continuing as
a grassy trail to another stile and gate
before fading out as you cross one of the
wider in a series of terraces. For the most
part, the route climbs straight up the hill,
the outlook across Loch Lomond and
further south to the Clyde improving
by the minute – with a far better view

LUSS

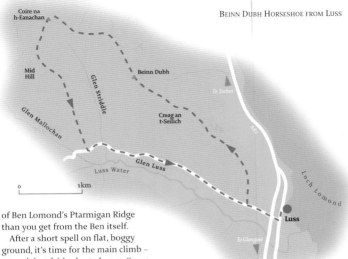

of Ben Lomond's Ptarmigan Ridge than you get from the Ben itself.

After a short spell on flat, boggy ground, it's time for the main climb – a tough but fairly short slog up Creag an t-Seilich. Wherever the track splits, take the most direct uphill option. After the next plateau, the track follows the fenceline, crossing it by a stile before flattening out and reaching a cairn. The best views are yet to come, however, as this is not the highest point on the ridge.

Here, the track heads NNW along the fenceline, dropping a little to give you a full dramatic picture of the Cobbler and the Arrochar Alps as well as the horseshoe-shaped ridge that lies ahead of you. Where the fence ends, continue in the same direction towards the Cobbler before striking west (left) across an open area of tussocky ground to gain the ridge by a faint trail just after a large patch of peat hags. This takes you to the summit cairn, with its sweeping views to the hills of Crianlarich.

Carry on past the cairn at Coire na h-Eanachan, following the vague track along the horseshoe ridge and down the shoulder of the hill towards Glen Luss. The descent can be steep at times, but is short-lived and never too difficult. Near the bottom, the very vague track comes to a stile over a fence. Take a direct line down from here towards a stone wall and gate. Climb this, and carry straight on down again over a final field. When you reach the barbed wire fence, turn right to locate a big gate onto the road after about 20m. Turn left to follow this road through Glen Luss back to the village, a pleasant tree-lined journey that takes around 30 minutes. Come off the road at the sign for the quarry path, following the trail up on the left to Luss via the footbridge again.

◂ Luss from the pier

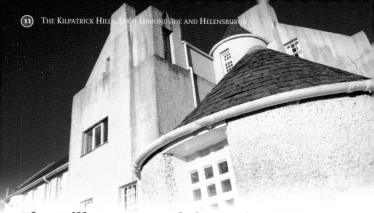

The Hill House and the Upland Way

Distance 10km **Time** 2 hours 30
Terrain tarmac roads (fairly steep at first)
and forest paths **Access** train from
Glasgow Queen Street to Helensburgh
Central or Upper Station

A visit to famed Glaswegian architect
Charles Rennie Mackintosh's Hill House
is easy to incorporate into this good
circular walk around Helensburgh.

This straightforward walk in a popular
town 'doon the watter' from Glasgow
offers no real route-finding issues,
starting just up from the pier and tourist
information building at Helensburgh
Central Station. Go straight up Sinclair
Street (B832) away from the seafront for
nearly 1.5km, passing Hermitage Park on
the right and Helensburgh Upper Station
– an alternative start point.

A few minutes past the train station,
where the road bends, turn left into
Kennedy Drive. A brown National Trust

for Scotland sign points the way to
the Hill House.

Turn right into Upper Colquhoun
Street to reach the main entrance.
A stroll around the gardens to admire
Mackintosh's architectural genius from
the outside is free, but it's well worth
paying the entrance fee for the house
itself (seasonal opening). Inside you'll
also find an afternoon tearoom.

Completed in 1904, the Hill House was
designed for wealthy Glasgow publisher
Walter Blackie and his family. By this time
Mackintosh had already created his iconic
Herald building (now The Lighthouse), as
well as the Glasgow School of Art and the
Willow Tearooms, but what makes the
Hill House extra special is that he also
had free rein with the interior – it is
'Mackintosh' inside and out, although
his artist wife Margaret MacDonald's
touches are also obvious inside.

To continue the walk, head further up

◀ The Hill House

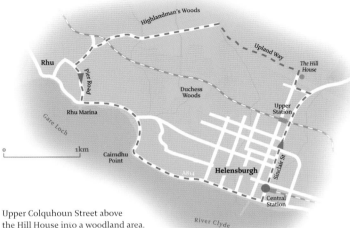

Rhu

Pier Road

Rhu Marina

Gare Loch

Cairndhu Point

Highlandman's Woods

Upland Way

The Hill House

Duchess Woods

Upper Station

Helensburgh

Sinclair St

A814

Central Station

River Clyde

0   1km

Upper Colquhoun Street above the Hill House into a woodland area.

Cross the car park at the top of the road and turn left, following a sign for Rhu Marina along a stony track and through a gate into a mix of woodland and open ground with a definite country feel. This track, known as the Upland Way, affords good views across to Glen Fruin to the north and south over Helensburgh itself, across the Clyde to Greenock and over to the Rosneath Peninsula on the other side of Gare Loch.

After crossing open ground, it continues through a gate and back into a large forested area made up of four woods – Drumfad Wood, Highlandman's Wood, Ardencaple Wood and Duchess Wood. At a signpost, head for Rhu Marina, 2.7km, to take a pretty path that winds through the trees, crossing several little bridges as it

rises gradually. It comes out at another sign for Rhu Marina, 2.5km, just past an ancient cup-marked boulder. Turn left to follow the long, straight Highlandman's Road all the way down towards Rhu and through a big metal gate, where there are expansive views to be had over Gare Loch to Rosneath. Carry on downhill with the tree-covered hillside to your right and fields below to emerge onto Station Road at Tor Farm. A 1km downhill stretch now follows, passing grand houses and lovely gardens, before turning left onto Pier Road which will take you down to the marina. Cross Gareloch Road here and turn left to return along the promenade to the town centre.

The Campsie Fells rise abruptly to the northeast of Glasgow, separating the northern suburbs of the city from the rolling Carse of Stirling. When viewed from the city, the steep southern escarpment slopes formed by the Campsie Fault appear as a sheer band of rock; above this is a rugged moorland plateau where there are few settlements.

Only two minor roads flow over the high ground from the south – the Crow Road twists its way from Lennoxtown to Fintry while at the tail-end of the Campsies, in the Kilsyth Hills, the Tak Ma Doon Road climbs from Kilsyth to Carron Bridge. Beneath the steep south face runs the broad, fertile Kelvin Valley where two green corridors – the River Kelvin, which rises in the Kilsyth Hills, and the historic Forth & Clyde Canal – eventually make their way into the heart of the city.

Beneath the western end of the Campsies, by the suburb of Milngavie, Mugdock Country Park is the venue for two very different walks. A popular family destination with lochs and woodland, castles, ponds and play areas, this also

contains the initial stretch of Scotland's most famous long-distance trail The West Highland Way, as well as the Glasgow version of the Khyber Pass.

This chapter also features several hill routes, including a walk from Blanefield to climb Dumgoyne, the iconic hill at the western end of the Campsies, the challenging Lecket Hill and Cort-ma Law, reached from Campsie Glen, the remote Meikle Bin, approached from Carron Valley, and the much easier Tomtain, accessed via the Tak Ma Doon Road above Kilsyth.

On the north side of the Kelvin Valley, Kilsyth is also the start point for a loop around Banton Loch, with the playpark and walled garden of the adjacent Colzium Estate perfect for younger families. On the southern slopes of the valley, Twechar marks the start of an undulating route that takes in the Roman fort on Bar Hill, following the Antonine Wall over Croy Hill before joining the canal just south of Kilsyth.

Almost all of these walks, ranging from one hour to half a day, are accessible by public transport.

Mugdock, the Campsies and Kelvin Valley

Mugdock and Dumbrock Loch

Distance 5km (+3km if starting at train
station) **Time** 1 hour 30 (+1 hour if
starting at train station) **Terrain** rough
and boggy ground, returning on good
paths and tracks **Map** OS Explorer 348
Access train from Glasgow to Milngavie;
follow West Highland Way from
Milngavie town centre; SPT's Ring'n'Ride
bus service is also available for this area

**An adventurous walk in the 750-acre
Mugdock Country Park to the north of
the city, passing lochs, historic castles
and woodland with great views of
Dumgoyne and the Campsies and a
return down the airy Khyber Pass.**

Start just north of the village of
Mugdock by the East Car Park in Mugdock
Country Park. Cross the road to enter by
a wooden gate on the right and follow
the faint line of worn ground NNE
towards a clump of trees. This shortly
passes through an old drystane dyke and
continues to an embankment where you
briefly follow a track left along the top
before it makes its rocky descent (can be

slippery) to a burn crossing. On the other
side, pick up the track again and continue
straight ahead to soon meet a road.

Cross this, heading towards the prow of
a small hill which the track now climbs
over. Where the track forks, ignore the
more obvious route veering right and take
the left branch which drops to cross a
patch of bog and passes through a
wooden gate at a drystane dyke onto a
well-defined stony track. Turn right here
for your first view of Dumbrock Loch,
which makes for an enjoyable shoreside
stroll with the distinctive hill of
Dumgoyne and the Campsies ahead right.

The track ends at a kissing gate
which you pass through and turn left

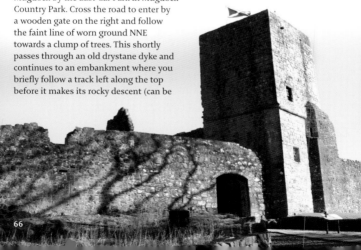

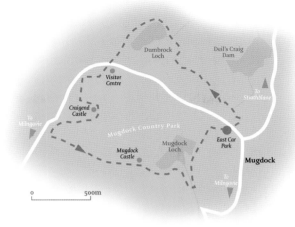

to accompany the fenceline over open ground above the loch and towards pylons. A good track soon appears, going uphill in the same direction. Take either track when it splits as both take you to a wooden gate and public road. Cross this to access Craigend Visitor Centre, which has a café, gift shop, playpark and walled gardens.

To continue, pass the visitor centre on the right and continue right past the playpark and then right again, along the lowest track, ignoring signs for Gallow Hill (unless you want to make a wee detour up it and then return to the route). At the ruined mansion of Craigend Castle, turn right, then right again at a junction, following the sign for Khyber Car Park.

This track emerges on a road at a gate. Turn left towards Mugdock Castle, with expansive views of the city ahead, the

Campsie Fells to your left and the Kilpatricks at your back. This is the Khyber Pass, a route used by Clydesiders to get away at weekends to the hills further north.

At the castle, go straight on, following a sign to the East Car Park and passing Mugdock Loch on the left as you enter lovely, secluded woodland. After the loch, take the first left across the bridge, signposted for the visitor centre. When you come to a junction, you can turn right for a direct return to the East Car Park or for a more interesting route which extends the adventure and gives a last view of the Campsies, cross straight over, ignoring both signposts, and take the smooth rocky path ahead to a stile. Beyond this, follow the track up the brae and take a right turn at the next junction before you head downhill to the car park.

◀ Mugdock Castle

On the Way to Carbeth

Distance 12km (+2km if starting at train station) **Time** 2 hours 30 (+30 mins if starting at train station) **Terrain** excellent paths, though can get muddy; some moderate climbs and a descent by cobbles and duckboards (sometimes slippery) **Map** OS Explorer 348 **Acccess** train from Glasgow to Milngavie; follow West Highland Way from Milngavie town centre; SPT's Ring'n'Ride bus service is also available for this area

A varied circuit in the popular Mugdock Country Park with good views and the chance to sample a scenic stretch of the West Highland Way.

Start at Drumclog Car Park by Mugdock Reservoir, just north of Milngavie. From here, follow signs for the West Highland Way – the popular 152km walking route from Milngavie to Fort William – picking up an excellent track that leads out over the top of Drumclog Moor. It's only a few minutes from the start point yet one of the best vantage spots of the entire walk. At the cross at the bottom of the hill, turn right for the West Highland Way.

Alternatively, to begin from Milngavie Station, follow signs to the start of the West Highland Way in the town centre, where the distinctive thistle markers direct you along a riverside path to Allander Park. At the edge of Drumclog Moor, by the cross at the bottom of the hill, this merges with the alternative start from the car park: carry straight on into Mugdock Wood.

A wide easygoing track winds its way alongside the Allander Water through this mossy oak wood, a protected Site of Special Scientific Interest. Where the track

meets a road, turn left onto this and follow it downhill to rejoin the track at a parking area opposite in 50m.

There are still plenty of trees around, but the views begin to open out from here – with the small but iconic peak of Dumgoyne pulling you on as you pass the still waters of Craigallian Loch on your right. Stay on this path to reach the hutting community at Carbeth, established in the pre-war years by Clydeside families escaping the city for some fresh air, with Carbeth Loch visible beyond. Just before the end of the huts (if you reach the main road, you've gone too far), pass through a gate on the right to follow a signed public footpath. The path over the hill can be hard going but any difficulties are short-lived. After 1km, turn right at a T-junction and stick to this main path as it snakes through woodland to a road, where you turn right and, after around 250m, left into Khyber Car Park. Go straight on, following the sign for Mugdock Castle, through a gate to join the Khyber Pass.

Go through another gate at the bottom of the pass and, after 100m, turn right via signs for the West Highland Way and Drumclog Moor. Before doing so, you might want to explore Mugdock Castle, a ruin with a long and eventful history dating back to the 13th century. Back on the walk, pass through an artfully constructed drystane dyke and descend by cobbled paths. Keep your ears open for woodpeckers as well as the calls of many other birds: this whole area is rich in wildlife, including deer.

Continue your descent on duckboards, turning left for the West Highland Way and Drumclog Moor. Turn left again at the bottom of the hill for the original path to the car park.

◄ Craigallian Loch and the distinctive top of Dumgoyne

Dumgoyne from Campsie Dene

Distance 10km **Time** 3 hours **Terrain** steep in places; good walking boots and stamina required **Map** OS Explorer 348 **Access** bus (10) from Buchanan Street Bus Station to Blanefield

The distinctive prow of Dumgoyne, a volcanic plug, has a special place in the hearts of hillwalkers from the Glasgow area. The fabulous views across the Campsies and to Ben Lomond and the Arrochar Alps are well worth the effort.

Begin from the war memorial at the start of Campsie Dene Road, which heads off the main street in Blanefield.

After around 2km, immediately past Cantywheery Cottage, the road crosses two bridges. Just before the second one, turn right off the road for access on to the hill through a gate.

A track winds steadily uphill, following the line of the trees of Craigbrock Wood and a burn on your left. The track will cross the burn higher up and head left towards Dumgoyne, so don't worry if you feel you're not heading in the right direction at the moment.

Take a welcome breather when the ground levels off to soak up the views and appreciate how much height you have already gained. At around 275m, you will have good views down past the wood and across the valley to Auchineden Hill and the Kilpatricks.

The track crosses the burn here, which poses no problems. Simply step across and head for a gap in the wall. Cross a

stile and pick up the track ahead, which passes beneath the steep-sided slopes of Dumfoyn – just 1m lower than Dumgoyne – and on towards the landmark peak itself. The path curves around the first hill, heading roughly northwest.

You will have been walking for about an hour or so before you reach the foot of Dumgoyne and begin the main climb. There are a number of tracks on the hill and yours will disappear for a short time, but just keep climbing and when you hit a main track, turn right to follow it all the way up to the top. The panoramic views from here are stunning – over to the nearby Earl's Seat and across the main Campsie ridge, as well as out to Ben Lomond and the Arrochar Alps. The Kilpatricks lie southwest across the valley.

To make a circuit of this walk, you can come down off the front of the hill, but there is one steep section so the less sure-footed may prefer to return the way they came. Otherwise, follow the path that can be seen leading down off the south side of the hill, traversing this until you see some worn paths on your right. Here, it's a wee bit loose underfoot and the slope is steep, but it's a well-used descent route.

As the slope eases, the track continues directly downhill to a wall. Cross over at a double stile and continue in a straight line across a field. Head between two trees to hit an old road above the main road. Glengoyne Distillery is close by on your right and there is a parking area near there for walkers tackling Dumgoyne directly up the route we have just come down.

On the old road, turn left. Follow it all the way back to the start. This stretch is around 4km long and will take nearly an hour, returning across the iron bridges, past Cantywheery Cottage and back down Campsie Dene Road.

◀ The iconic peak of Dumgoyne

Lecket Hill and Cort-ma Law

Distance 10km **Time** 3 hours 30
Terrain mostly hill paths; steep section
to reach Lecket Hill; map and compass
required as well as decent navigation
skills **Map** OS Explorer 348 **Access** bus
(X85) from Glasgow to Clachan of Campsie

Within just half an hour of the city,
this walk gives a wonderful sense of
escape and a taste for the novice walker
of what to expect on the bigger hills of
Scotland. This circuit crosses an evocative
and windswept landscape with great
views, but it can also get very wet and
boggy, so go well prepared.

In Clachan of Campsie, a designated
Conservation Area near Lennoxtown,
head north round the back of the row
of shops to pass Old St Machan's Church
and graveyard on your left.

A fitting tribute cairn to the late writer,
broadcaster and mountaineer Tom Weir
marks the start of Weir's Way up the glen.
Follow this gravel path all the way up to
an information point, where you branch
right to get to the large 'car park in the
sky' by the curve in the Crow Road: this
section will take about an hour.

From here, you carry on up the rising
Crow Road, taking care of traffic, for
around 1.5km. Look for the burn and
parking space on the right and then the
path which is 150m or so further on, also
on the right. This path takes the best line

up Lecket Hill with a steep climb to start, but bear with it as it will soon level off and not much more ascent will be needed. Once you gain the cairn that signals the top of Lecket Hill, you can commend yourself on how high you've risen above the city to your south.

The next destination is Cort-ma Law (Law being an old Scots word for hill) and, for some, venturing into this kind of terrain can be quite daunting. Frequently used by orienteers and by mountain guides for training, this landscape can be disorientating if you are not used to it and very tiring in poor weather. Taking the relevant OS map and a compass with you is always a good idea.

Head roughly southeast over tufted, undulating moorland to the Cort-ma Law trig point, which can be seen from some distance on the skyline. At 531m above sea level, this is the highest point on the route and in fine weather a great view of the city unfolds beneath you here.

From the top, a path follows the ridge west for 1km or so to reach the cairn that marks the top of Lairs, the views to the south and west greatly rewarding that strenuous initial ascent to Lecket Hill. Continuing on a good path in the same direction, you start to descend, ever more rapidly until the path slants off leftwards to bring you out on the road, close to the car park. Return to the start.

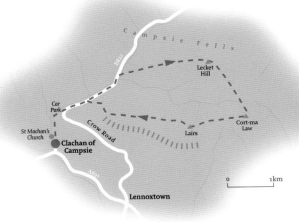

Mighty Meikle Bin

**Distance 12.5km Time 3 hours 30
Terrain mostly excellent forestry roads
with grassy trails later on and a couple of
very wet and boggy stretches; open,
exposed ascent Map OS Explorer 348
Access no public transport to this walk;
limited parking**

**Venture up the back of the Campsies to
the remote and lofty Meikle Bin,
enjoying views across central Scotland
to the Southern Highlands from the
distinctive double bump at its summit.**

Start at Todholes, near the head of the
Carron Valley Reservoir on the B818 east
of Fintry. Don't block farm or forestry
access roads if arriving by car.

A green metal barrier at the end of a
forestry road marks the gateway to Meikle
Bin. It's a gentle start on this excellent
forestry road, which is fringed by orchids

and foxgloves in summer, and the Carron
Valley Reservoir gradually comes into
view as you ascend into pine forest. Keep
to the forestry road as it bears left near
the water, ignoring a road to the right.

Meikle Bin – Scots for 'big hill' –
soon appears before you. After crossing a
concrete bridge over a large burn, take the
second track to the right (at the point
where the main road bends uphill to the
left). This slightly overgrown track leads
through a plantation to eventually arrive
at a small grassy plateau with fantastic
views of the Trossachs and Ben Lomond.

A small track now takes you uphill on
the left, becoming very muddy under the
trees before emerging onto the open
hillside. Continue climbing on the
obvious desire line which leads steeply up
the shoulder of Meikle Bin. At a slight dip
just before the final ascent, you'll see the

◀ The sun going down over Meikle Bin

wreckage of a Firefly plane which came down here in the 1950s, killing the two navy airmen aboard.

On reaching the top you will be rewarded with some stunning 360-degree views. The Wallace Monument, Grangemouth refinery and Edinburgh Castle can all be seen, as well as down to Kintyre, the peaks of Arran and Dumfriesshire too.

To descend, head straight off the summit in the opposite direction to which you gained it, towards Glasgow. This initially vague path gains definition as it leads down open slopes into a firebreak.

Shortly after crossing a couple of ditches – one is muddy, the second has wooden sleepers across it to aid walkers – turn left into a firebreak. Here, the track can get boggy before you emerge from the forest and pick up another decent desire line, dipping down and up right towards a small turning area. Join what becomes a good downhill track heading roughly eastwards from here. At a junction go right, heading away from the hill, on what is now a very good forestry road.

At the first fork after this, carry straight on ahead, ignoring a forestry road to the left. At the second split, turn left over a bridge, noticing ancient shielings on your left as you make your way on a long but easy wooded stretch which eventually runs alongside the reservoir. After passing an old quarry on your left and a picnic area near the water, you come to a large junction. Turn right to follow the road back to the start.

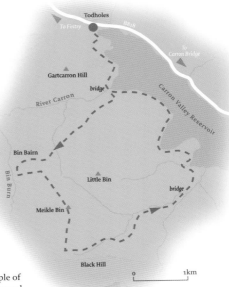

Todholes
To Fintry
B818
To Carron Bridge
Gartcarron Hill
bridge
River Carron
Carron Valley Reservoir
Bin Bairn
Bin Burn
Little Bin
bridge
Meikle Bin
Black Hill
0   1km

Tak me up tae Tomtain

Distance 3km **Time** 40 mins **Terrain** fairly
steep open ground, can be boggy
Map OS Explorer 348 **Access** Kilsyth is
easily reached by bus (27, 24) from
Buchanan Street Bus Station, but the car
park at the start of the walk is a 4km walk
up the Tak ma Doon Road which is steep,
narrow and twisty with no pavement

Despite being such a short walk, a trip up
Tomtain is very rewarding, even for those
who prefer bigger mountains. Giving
commanding views from east to west,
with the Forth Bridges often visible from
the summit, this is one of those very few
places where it's possible to gain a
spectacular overview of the area for
little effort.

Tomtain is reached by taking the steep,
narrow and bendy Tak ma Doon Road out
of Kilsyth. Just as the road levels off,
you'll see a large car park on your right,
which marks the start of your walk.
Around 300m on from this, as you round
a little bend, you'll see a large galvanised
steel barrier and the start of a path.

As you are already at around 310m, the
walk up the 453m-high Tomtain is pretty
easy and certainly involves little effort for
the quality of the views you'll be
rewarded with. The actual walk from the
road to the top of Tomtain – clearly
visible on the ridge to the west – is a
gentle incline giving a grand perspective
over the region stretching from the Forth
to the Clyde and from Stirlingshire to
Dumfriesshire. There should be no
navigation issues, as a good path
accompanies a fence and a drystane dyke,
the latter an excellent navigational

◄ The trig point on top of Tomtain

handrail, from the barrier at the start.

The path begins at a very pleasant gradient with nice open views out to the east and across to the Forth, the Lothians and the Pentlands. You can also see as far down as Tinto in Lanarkshire. Across the rough, rounded moor, the path maintains a steady incline but can be a bit muddy at times. There's a fabulous array of wildflowers, including bog myrtle, as well as small birds, butterflies and moths fluttering all around in the summer months – a surprising amount of life for what at first seems to be barren moorland.

As the bulge of Tomtain looms before you, the path begins to steepen in stages and the Ochils, Wallace Monument and Stirling Castle come into view as well as Carron Valley Reservoir to the Gargunnocks. This is also a good walk to do in the winter when clearer, colder days can extend the views as far as the Cheviots to the south and Ben More and Stob Binnein around Crianlarich, but it must be said it also offers little shelter from any inclement weather.

To return, retrace your steps or to extend this walk simply carry on along the ridge past Tomtain to Garrel Hill which, at 459m, is slightly higher, though not such a distinct top.

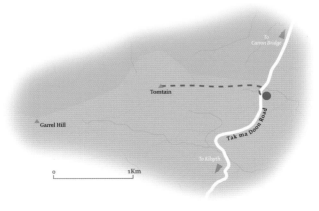

Tomtain

Garrel Hill

To Carron Bridge

Tak ma Doon Road

To Kilsyth

0   1Km

Banton Loch and Colzium

Distance 7km **Time** 2 hours **Terrain** level lochside, forest and farm tracks with some rougher field crossings. Younger families will find short entertaining walks in the Colzium Estate **Access** bus (27, 24) from Buchanan Street Bus Station to Stirling Road through Kilsyth

A level circuit of Banton Loch whose peaceful air belies its bloody history as the site of the 1645 Battle of Kilsyth. This walk starts and finishes in Kilsyth's delightful Colzium Lennox Estate.

Located on the site of a castle built for the Earl of Lennox in the 12th century, the estate has many points of interest, including an excellent children's playground, picnic spots and summer tearoom, arboretum, 18th-century mansion and curling pond, clock theatre, aviary, a wonderful walled garden and a wild glen of tumbling waterfalls, mossy rocks and ferns.

It is Banton Loch (Townhead Reservoir), adjacent to the Estate, though, which provides the setting for much of this walk. Here, the bloody Battle of Kilsyth took place in 1645, where more than 4000 Covenanters, under the command of Lieutenant-General Baillie, met their deaths at the hands of a smaller army of Royalists, under James Graham, Marquis of Montrose. Bones and armoury are still being found in the fields to the north of the loch to this day.

Start from the entrance to the park on Stirling Road, where you'll see a tarmac road heading eastwards, parallel to the main road. Bear right onto this to enter a

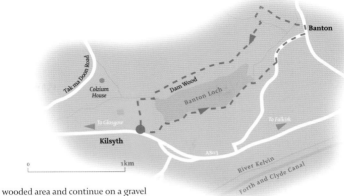

wooded area and continue on a gravel surface, where a sign soon directs you to Banton via Banton Loch. On reaching the loch, take the path around the right-hand side for Banton. At the road end, where there is a memorial to the Battle of Kilsyth, cross a bridge over a water outlet to follow a gently meandering lochside path. This passes under a canopy of mature forestry to emerge by some dwellings and a gate onto Banton Road. Head left up the road through the pretty village of Banton to a crossroads with a postbox on one corner and the Swan Inn on another. Turn left to leave town, shortly passing a Baptist church where you bear left onto a farm access road, signed for Auchinrivoch Farm.

This winds its way uphill to a junction at Wester Auchinrivoch Farm, where a left turn takes you onto the site of the battle. A gentle descent, contouring left, then right, follows. Where the road bends uphill to the right, carry straight on into a field (keep dogs on a tight lead).

Continue in the same direction as you were on the road to pick up a path at the bottom of this field. On the other side of the field, this becomes clearer, passing between an old stone dyke and a fence to reach a gate and a tricky stile.

As you approach a forest with a broken wall on to your right and a carpet of wildflowers all around in summer, the views across the loch and over to Bar Hill open up: this is a fine place for peaceful contemplation. At the top corner of the forest, a track leads into the eerie Dam Wood: follow this, ignoring any offshoots, to continue through an old wrought-iron gate and across a bridge to a signed junction back by the loch. A right turn for Colzium Lennox Estate brings you to the main driveway after 150m, where it's a choice between returning to the entrance on the left or a whole big park to explore straight ahead.

◀ Memorial to the Marquis of Montrose in Colzium Estate

Bar Hill and the Antonine Wall

Distance 9km **Time** 2 hours 30
Terrain good canal towpath, rough farm track and open hill. Some steep sections
Access buses (X27, 87, 184) from Buchanan Street Bus Station to Twechar

This walk traces the Antonine Wall, once the northern boundary of the Roman Empire, from the remains of a fort and bathhouse on Bar Hill through woodland to Croy Hill, before a meandering return along one of the most scenic stretches of the Forth & Clyde Canal.

Begin at the village of Twechar, between Kilsyth and Kirkintilloch. A Historic Scotland sign near the Barrhill Tavern on the Main Street points the way up a rough farm track to the Bar Hill fort and Antonine Wall. Be warned, the sign is a little optimistic with the distance given.

The track rises gently, giving increasingly good views down to the Forth & Clyde Canal and the Kilsyth Hills. After about 1km, just before you reach a domed reservoir, go through a gate on your left to reach the top of Bar Hill. The remains of the Roman fort and bathhouse lie just over the brow of the hill. A large collection of coins was found when this site was excavated, suggesting it was also something of a gambling den.

Looking down the hill with its commanding views, the Antonine Wall lies about 60m away. This old stone and turf rampart is of great historic importance, having been built between 142 and 143AD on the orders of Emperor Antoninus Pius. Stretching some 60km from Bo'ness in the east to Old Kilpatrick in the west, it was the northern frontier of the Roman Empire for around 20 years before the legions retreated south.

Drop down to the wall, and follow it east towards a large clearing. As you approach dense trees, it gets a little rough underfoot, but continue along the wall and fenceline to contour round to the left towards the clearing. From here, the wall

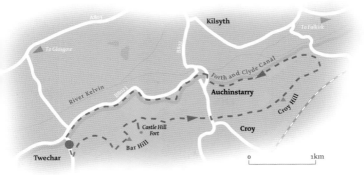

stretches down the hill before you (to your right a track climbs to the small Iron Age fort on Castle Hill, also in the care of Historic Scotland and worth a detour).

To continue the walk, descend eastwards along the line of the Antonine Wall until you reach a stone wall. Turn right, then left, picking up a landrover track after about 40m which goes through gates to join the main Auchinstarry to Croy road. To shorten the walk, you can turn left to join the canal at Auchinstarry. Otherwise, go straight over the road and through a painted green metal gate to cross a rough field, keeping close to a barbed wire fence on your right. After 300m, at a green gate by a tiny substation, turn right on a tarmac-surfaced road towards houses and signposts for Croy Hill.

Climb the hill, keeping to the left-hand track closest to the edge when it splits beyond the houses. The Antonine Wall gains definition as you ascend and the views over the valley and to the Kilsyth Hills and the Campsies open out once

again. There is no obvious summit to Croy Hill – which has the remains of a Roman fortlet just beneath it – and there's a network of trails on top. For ease, take the central track that heads eastwards between the two mini peaks and, as you start to descend, pick up another trail which heads sharply (almost 90 degrees) down to the valley and canal below, passing a copse of several mature trees and a large fallen tree. In summer, dense growth may make this trail difficult to pick out, but it soon becomes a proper track which leads all the way down to the canal and its towpath, and then to Auchinstarry Basin with its many colourful barges and boats.

Cross the canal at Auchinstarry via the roadbridge, and turn immediately left through the black and white barrier to pick up the canal towpath. This gives a pleasant tree-lined ramble to Twechar, a contrast to the earlier rough ground. On reaching the village, return over the roadbridge to the Main Street.

◀ Wash day on the Forth & Clyde Canal

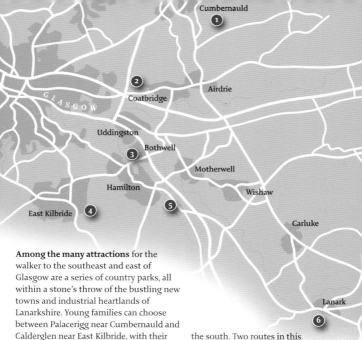

Among the many attractions for the walker to the southeast and east of Glasgow are a series of country parks, all within a stone's throw of the bustling new towns and industrial heartlands of Lanarkshire. Young families can choose between Palacerigg near Cumbernauld and Calderglen near East Kilbride, with their nature trails, adventure playgrounds and children's zoos. At Drumpellier Country Park near Coatbridge, you can combine an easy trail around the loch with a quiet walk in the woods, while at Chatelherault Country Park by Hamilton, a great trail follows the Avon Water, a tributary of the Clyde, across bridges and gorges, past a ruined castle and through an ancient oak woodland.

Another Lanarkshire highlight is the lush Clyde Valley with its riverside walkway extending for 65km from the centre of Glasgow to the Falls of Clyde in the south. Two routes in this chapter follow sections of the walkway. One circuit starts from the village of Blantyre, childhood home of David Livingstone, to explore a stretch of the Clyde, a dramatic ruined castle and the leafy village of Bothwell. Further south, a walk from the historic cotton mills of the New Lanark World Heritage Site climbs nature trails above the spectacular Falls of Clyde, returning through a wildlife reserve.

All of the walks in this chapter, with the exception of New Lanark, can be completed in two hours and most are accessible by bus or train.

'The Keep' at Calderglen Country Park ▶

Clyde Valley and Lanarkshire

Palacerigg and Fannyside Loch

Distance 7km **Time** 1 hour 30
Terrain excellent tracks most of the
way but moorland trails can get muddy;
Treetop Walkway involves steps and
requires a head for heights!
Access train from Glasgow Queen
Street to Cumbernauld (2.5km away)

**This rewarding circuit of Palacerigg
Country Park near Cumbernauld begins
from the visitor centre and children's
farmyard before picking up an adventure
playground-style treetop walkway and
nature and moorland trails.**

Palacerigg makes for a great family day
out, with its collection of farmyard
animals including rare breeds such as
Boreray Sheep and Scots Dumpy chickens,
as well as some black swans, and a
playpark. It is also a terrific countryside
resource, with 300 hectares of woodland,
moorland, grassland and ponds which
support rich wildlife, with an emphasis
on environmental education. Founded in
the early 1970s, a beautiful mural by the
Glasgow writer and artist Alasdair Gray
inside the visitor centre is dedicated to
the naturalist who planned the park.

Starting from the visitor centre, exit the
car park on the road you would have
entered by until you see a metal gate and
signpost just after a speed bump on the
left. Turn up this track, following signs for
the Laverock Trail and the Treetop
Walkway and, at a wooden sign on the left
after about 50m, leave the main track for
the Treetop Walkway. This is exactly as
described and might bring on a touch of
vertigo in some – but handrails and wire
netting make it perfectly safe and it is
great fun. Climb the steps onto an
adventure playground-style elevated
wooden walkway and enjoy a bird's eye
view of the canopy as you wind your way
among the trees.

On reaching the end of this feature, turn

◀ Moorland at Palacerigg

right to return to the main track and then head left. You leave this main track again soon, when you come to a sign for the Laverock Nature Trail (marked by posts with green rings) on your right. This grassy track, filled with wildflowers in summer, winds its way narrowly through ferns, past richly-scented orchids and through a pine forest.

Eventually you emerge on a bigger track where you pick up the signposted Toddlemoor Trail, marked throughout with posts with blue rings as it rambles across open moor, giving views over rolling farmland. This trail ends at a gateway after around 10 minutes: turn left to head straight down a red-surfaced landrover track, passing a field and the

corner of the golf course. Ignore a turn-off here and continue straight ahead to pass Fannyside Loch on your right, where there's a wee trail down to the water for those wanting to explore further.

Around here, the views begin to open out with the pointy peak of Meikle Bin often visible in the distance. After the track bends to the left, it splits, with an option to cut across the golf course. Go right to skirt around the golf course, then carry on ahead, ignoring a turn-off for Abronhill and keeping straight at the next junction to steer away from the golf course. At a natural bend at the end of a long stretch of road, follow signs for the Park Centre to eventually arrive at a tarmac road and cattle grid.

Turn left here to return to the visitor centre, with its animal pens, playpark and welcoming café.

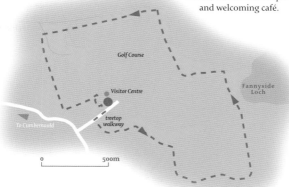

Golf Course

Visitor Centre

Fannyside Loch

To Cumbernauld

treetop walkway

0   500m

Exploring Drumpellier

Distance 5km **Time** 1 hour 30
Terrain mostly level; tarmac walkways,
particularly around loch, and good
woodland tracks with muddy patches
and some gates **Access** train from
Glasgow Queen Street to Blairhill Station
near Blair Road entrance

A tour of the popular Drumpellier
Country Park near Coatbridge which
combines a long ramble through quiet
woodland with the well-trodden loop
around Lochend Loch, its family-friendly
attractions, visitor centre and café.

Drumpellier has two natural lochs:
Woodend Loch is a protected SSSI (Site of
Special Scientific Interest), while Lochend
Loch is the focal point for entertainment
in the park, with paddle-boating, play
parks and geese and ducks. In medieval
times, Drumpellier was the farming
grange of the Newbattle Abbey monks,
and was bought in the 1700s by Andrew

Buchanan, later Glasgow Lord Provost,
and turned into landscaped pleasure
grounds and parkland. It was gifted to the
people of Coatbridge in 1919 and officially
designated a country park in 1984.

If your visit is on a nice day, particularly
during the school holidays, you won't be
alone. Popular with daytrippers since the
early part of last century, it is nevertheless
fairly easy to find peace and quiet in the
500 acres of parkland.

Start your walk from the visitor centre,
accessed off Townhead Road if arriving by
car, and go anti-clockwise around the
water by an excellent tarmac walkway.
Rail travellers can start the route from
Blairhill Station, a 30-minute walk from
the visitor centre.

The walk around the loch is called
the Crannog Circuit as the loch was
once home to a 'crannog', an Iron Age
defensive dwelling that sat on stilts on
open water, now just marked by buoys.

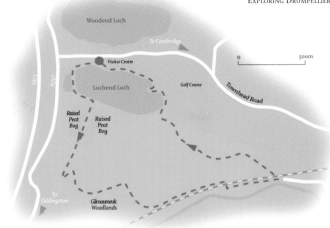

You'll also pass ponds, with waterfowl and reedbeds, and plenty of wildflowers in summer.

As the walkway straightens out on the far side of the loch, a board marked 'A Walk in the Wood' directs you right, up a long tree-lined avenue. Carry straight on at a junction to follow the fingerpost sign for the Raised Bog Walk. This turns sharply left after about 1km before turning right after another 200m to enter Gilmourneuk Woods, where you'll see an established circle of trees up ahead.

The path goes up over a slight rise to round this copse of trees before heading down a long straight, wiggling its way over a few mounds and bumps with views over the nearby towns. On the downhill, take a right turn towards an old treeline where you'll see a small ruin on the right. The path then veers left and runs

alongside a fence and railway siding where it can be muddy underfoot, before entering a wooded area – a good place to spot foxes. Go past a metal barrier and continue straight along the track to meet a red-surfaced path at a sharp bend. Follow this to the right, cross a railway bridge and turn left to follow a gravel track alongside the railway and you will eventually meet a road.

Turn left to follow the road under the railway and all the way back to the visitor centre (or carry on straight ahead to join Blair Road and catch your train at Blairhill Station). The path returns through a mix of open ground and woodland, passing playing fields on your right and a nursery and gardens on your left before going through a kissing gate to Lochend Loch and the path back to the visitor centre and car park.

Blantyre and Bothwell Castle

Distance 5km **Time** 1 hour 30
Terrain roads, pavements and good forest
trails make this easy underfoot though it
can be a bit muddy **Access** train from
Glasgow Central to Blantyre Station; the
route can also be started easily from the
centre of Bothwell

**A riverside ramble through woodland
from the David Livingstone Centre in
Blantyre, with detours to a 13th-century
castle and the leafy village of Bothwell.**

From Blantyre Station, head straight
along Station Road. Near the end, you'll
see some black iron gates to the David
Livingstone Centre on the left. Run by the
National Trust for Scotland, there is a fee
to enter the museum dedicated to the
great missionary and explorer who grew
up in Blantyre, but those choosing not to
visit should still stop to see the incredible
bronze sculpture just inside the grounds.

About 200m further down the road,
you'll come to the cantilevered David
Livingstone Memorial footbridge.
It occupies a scenic spot over the Clyde,
the waters appearing green from the
reflection of trees. This was the site of the
first footbridge between the villages of
Blantyre and Bothwell, replacing an old
ferry service when it was built in 1852.
When the water levels are low, a weir and
a fish ladder can be seen to the right. Once
over, you turn immediately left through a
metal gate onto the start of a fine
riverside walk along a pretty, wooded
stretch of the river. A small crag on your
right bears a chiselled inscription marking
the level that the waters reached during a
disastrous flood in 1782. In less than 1km,
the path starts to rise and leave the river:
follow this (ignoring a waterside
subsidiary path) to a junction behind a
housing estate. Go left, returning
gradually downhill towards the riverbank.

After around 1km, the red ruins

◀ Bothwell Castle

of Bothwell Castle come dramatically into view. Within the castle grounds, there's a Historic Scotland visitor centre and it's easy to reach by car, but this river path gives a far more memorable first glimpse of the well-preserved ruins, said to be the best surviving example of a 13th-century castle in Scotland. It changed hands a number of times and had a notable role in the Wars of Independence – being captured and recaptured by the English and the Scots, and even being dismantled after Bannockburn in a bid to deter the English from further occupation. Particular notice should be drawn to the circular donjon at one end and the traces of a moat that once surrounded it. The sprawling lawns make a lovely spot for a picnic.

Retrace your steps to the junction behind the housing estate. Instead of turning right downhill, carry straight on by the estate for some time before heading back into the woods. At a fork, go left to maintain height and left again at the next small junction. The woodland boundary wall can be seen on your right as you ramble pleasantly uphill to emerge on a main road at some gates. Turn right to reach the corner of Blantyre Mill Road after 25m. A right turn onto this road will

take you back to the footbridge and station beyond, but it is worth turning left to visit Bothwell.

The village developed in the 19th century as wealthy Glasgow traders began to settle here on the advice of their doctors, who lauded the benefits of its clear air and water. There are many impressive Victorian mansions to be seen around here and the Main Street, located at the top of Blantyre Mill Road, is a good spot for a drink or bite to eat. You can also pay a visit to the oldest collegiate church in Scotland by bearing right onto Main Street and then left onto Green Street. The beautiful Bothwell Parish Church was founded in 1398 by Archibald 'the Grim', resident of Bothwell Castle. Retrace your steps to the start.

89

Calderglen river walk

Distance 7km **Time** 1 hour 30
Terrain mostly level with some steps;
good forest paths and plenty of
attractions make this suitable for
families of all ages **Access** regular train
from Glasgow Central to East Kilbride;
bus (20) from Glasgow Union Street stops
on Strathaven Road (a 10-minute walk
from park entrance)

An amble through lush woodland in
East Kilbride's popular Calderglen
Country Park, following trails high up
among the trees in the enchanting
Calder Glen and returning to the
children's zoo, conservatory and
ornamental gardens. This route can be
extended to incorporate the raised bog
of Langlands Moss.

From the entrance to the park off
Strathaven Road, follow the driveway up
to the visitor centre and main car park.
Take the path alongside the conservatory,
following the sign for 'Nature trails and
adventure play area' to reach a map board.
Turn right here, signed Tor Trail, watching
out for the small yellow flower icon that
accompanies this trail. Passing a gap in
the hedge to your right, you will spy the
impressive 14th-century Torrance House.
One of old East Kilbride's original
buildings, it now houses a museum and
café. Below to the left, long grassy banks
tumble down to an adventure playground
and you'll pass several picnic tables as you
accompany the yellow flower signs
into the undergrowth.

Here, you start to descend, ignoring a
sign for a barbecue site, Horseshoe Falls
and the Tor Trail and instead taking a
small trail off to the right to dive further
into undergrowth and alongside a

◀ Autumn in Calderglen

wooden railing into Calder Glen.
A lofty trail ambles above this very
pretty wooded ravine, with the
river and its series of small
waterfalls far below.

In time, the path drops
down to a junction. From
here, it is possible to
extend the walk out to
the raised bog of
Langlands Moss,
an ecologically
important site for
plant and insect
life (signposted).
Alternatively, turn left to
cross the river by the
attractive South Bridge and
climb some steps to return
along the opposite bank of
the Rotten Calder.

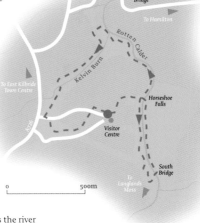

After 10 minutes or so, cross the river
by a large bridge and maintain your
course, keeping to the lower path before
following it uphill away from the water
and back down some steps on the right
(all marked by the yellow flower). You
now leave the main path to return to the
riverside, undulating gently through the
woods and crossing a couple of wooden
bridges. Carry on along the main path by
a fence. When it emerges onto the main
access road into the park, turn left,
crossing the bridge to pick up the Tor Trail
on the other side. Stick to the main track
and you will eventually arrive back at the

car park not far from the entrance.
The children's zoo, conservatory and
ornamental gardens, located here, are
well worth exploring. The little zoo is
great, with the meerkats, wolf-whistling
thrush and guinea pigs among its
particular attractions. In the conservatory,
there are lush plants as well as pythons,
chameleons, tropical fish, birds, prairie
dogs and cheeky marmoset monkeys to
enchant the kids while the ornamental
gardens outside are beautifully kept.

Chatelherault and the Avon Gorge

Distance 8km **Time** 2 hours **Terrain** good forest tracks throughout; can get muddy in places and there are a couple of steeper sections and flights of steps **Access** train from Glasgow Central to Chatelherault

Take a long walk in the woods at Chatelherault Country Park near Hamilton, starting from an impressive 18th-century hunting lodge – now a visitor centre – high on the hill overlooking the town to pass a ruined castle, ancient oak trees and a pretty river gorge.

As you enter the park by the main entrance, you'll notice an excellent children's adventure playground and a garden centre before you reach the car park and the main attraction here – the 18th-century hunting lodge built for the Duke of Hamilton, who also held the title Duc de Chatelherault. What is now a 500-acre country park was once part of the Duke's estates.

Facing the main entrance to the visitor centre (the old lodge), follow the wide path (signed Cadzow Oaks) immediately left to head down through tall redwood trees behind the lodge before bending sharply left and downhill at another sign for Cadzow Oaks. The path soon crosses the Duke's Bridge, 30m above the Avon Water. Here, the ruins of Cadzow Castle, a royal residence up to the time of Robert the Bruce, appear on your right.

Carry straight on up a slight incline before entering woodland: the route follows the smaller trail to the left of the estate road beside the castle. On meeting another path, turn left for an easy, level amble under the canopy. A sign soon appears for the Duke's Monument to the right, an interesting 1.7km detour (one way) for those who want to extend their tour. Alternatively, continue straight on to Cadzow Oaks, reached by a few steps on your right. These gnarly trees, dated back to 1444 by their ring marks, look like they

◂ The Duke of Hamilton's
hunting lodge

could spring to life at any moment. Like the castle, they bear the old name for Hamilton: Cadzow was renamed in 1445 with the permission of King James II. This is a good spot for a picnic or to let youngsters play and explore.

On the other side of the copse, in line with the fence, rejoin the path and continue uphill into the main forest. An undulating tree-lined stretch follows, with a couple of relatively steep sections and a brief foray into an open patch of ground (a tapestry of wildflowers in summer), before retreating back under the tree canopy. At a Y-junction, stick to the main path as it continues through the wood, widening on its descent to Green Bridge. Like the Duke's Bridge, this is a lovely feature, crossing the Avon Water at a wide, shallow stretch where you'd be forgiven for thinking you were in the heart of Perthshire. A stone-arched bridge slightly upstream completes the picture.

After crossing, head straight up into the trees via a stony track and long flight of steps, ignoring the track closer to the riverbank. At a fork, take the higher path on the right to return to the main entrance to the visitor centre. Grand as it is, this building – which now houses a good café, exhibition gallery and shop – was not the Duke of Hamilton's main residence. That was the nearby Hamilton Palace, sadly long demolished due to subsidence. The lodge was built by renowned architect William Adam, but was really little more than a glorified kennel for hunting dogs. It also has a bit of an affliction: quarrying took place in front of the house in the last century and the subsequent subsidence has left visitors feeling a wee bit off-balance in some of the rooms.

93

New Lanark and the Falls of Clyde

Distance 10km **Time** 3 hours **Terrain** good
paths throughout with duckboards at the
start; undulating with occasional steep
sections, some steps and drops
Access train from Glasgow Central to
Lanark (2.5km away); shuttle bus to
New Lanark Visitors' Car Park

**This walk begins and ends at the World
Heritage Site of New Lanark, following
the River Clyde to take in a series of
spectacular waterfalls.**

The picturesque cotton mill community
of New Lanark, which represented Robert
Owen's 19th-century socialist utopia, with
decent housing, free healthcare, night
classes for workers and Britain's first
infant school, today combines a brilliantly
restored early industrial environment
with spectacular natural surroundings.

Start from the main car park above New
Lanark World Heritage Site. Walk downhill
into the heart of the village and head left
past the visitor centre and café. Water was
routed down here for the old mills: follow
the walkway upstream beside it. Climb
some stone steps and head away from the
buildings, signed Clyde Walkway and Falls
of Clyde, to climb another flight of

steps up into trees above the River Clyde.
Returning to the water, there is a long
stretch of duckboards where a viewpoint
over a small weir system – this is Dundaff
Linn – gives a taste of what is to come.
At a fork, stick to the waterside to reach
Bonnington Power Station.

Soon, you climb to the viewpoint at
Corra Linn: the falls are particularly
impressive in spate and part of a
landscape that dates back to the Ice Age.
The celebrated Romantic landscape artist
JMW Turner painted the falls in 1840 and
writers have also made their pilgrimage
here, among them Sir Walter Scott and
the poets Coleridge and Wordsworth.

Climb the steps above the viewpoint,
following the sign for Bonnington Linn
and stick to the high path all the way

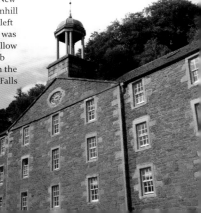

Lanark

Kirkfieldbank

Castlebank

New Lanark
Visitor
Centre

Power Station

Castle
ruins
Corra Linn

River Clyde

Bonnington
Linn

0   1km

there. Although not quite as grand as Corra Linn, this upper part of the Falls of Clyde system is still lovely. Cross the new bridge just past here, and turn right down the opposite side of the river towards the Wildlife Reserve. Where the main path veers away from the river, pick up a smaller one to gain height above the tumbling waters of Bonnington Linn. Keeping to the path closest to the river, pass the remains of the fortified 13th-century Corra Castle, home to an important bat colony: intruders are liable to a hefty fine. Very soon the path passes the falls at Corra Linn. There's a great vantage point here, but around 15m down a path leads to a tiny promontory right over the cascade.

The path continues past the Wildlife Reserve on your left and then New Lanark across the water at roughly the halfway point, before eventually emerging at a road and houses. Turn right downhill to follow a sign back to the Clyde Walkway at the bottom right. An old humpback bridge leads to a collection of houses, where you should turn right again through a gate: don't be deterred by a sign declaring CCTV coverage; this is a public right of way.

Beyond the gate, head toward the water, passing through another gate to pick up a grassy trail along the riverside. After going through a small swing gate, cross a road at a water treatment works and climb a steeper path with steps ahead. Turn right at some farm buildings to continue on a tarmac road with airy views. Near a bend in the road, opposite Rubislaw Cottage, turn right through a gateway into Castlebank Park. Follow the red walkway, passing a grotto on your left, until a small green sign points to the Clyde Walkway on the right. Follow this back to the riverside, before crossing a bridge and climbing once again to emerge on the road through New Lanark.

◀ The mills at New Lanark

Index